BENNETT STREET SUNDAY SCHOOL

1801 – 1966

A Manchester History

M W LEES

Published in 2013 by:

Stellar Books LLP
Dunham Gatehouse
Charcoal Road
Bowdon
Cheshire
WA14 4RY

www.stellarbooks.co.uk

Designed and edited by Patricia C Byron of Stellar Books

Printed by Deanprint Ltd, Stockport, Cheshire.

ISBN: 978-0956508959

Contents

Dedication

This history is affectionately dedicated to the memory of 'the Clan', just one example of the lasting friendships forged at Bennett Street. This group was formed in 1926 and met monthly for over fifty years for Sunday tea and discussion, pledging to assist each other in times of trouble.

Henry Timperley 1906-1971
Thomas Lowe (Tom) 1906-1971
Albert Edward Chadwick (Bert) 1906-1975
Arthur Noel Cox 1904-1980
Rowley Dalton Fletcher 1905-1980
Edmund Grundy Lees 1906-1993; my father. He outlived these close friends by thirteen years and greatly missed their comradeship.

But most particularly this work has been written for Rowley Fletcher, Bennett Street's last secretary, who in his later years voiced his regret that a history of the school had not been produced.

Acknowledgements

This history of Bennett Street Sunday School originates from a dissertation '*A study of two large Sunday schools in the Manchester region during the Victoria and Edwardian eras*' which was submitted in partial fulfilment of the requirement for the degree of MA in the History of the Manchester Region at Manchester Metropolitan University in 2001. It was supervised by John Mason whose guidance was acknowledged both then and is now. I am grateful too to Terry Wyke my tutor during the course for his advice on earlier drafts of this present work.

Professor Derek P Torrington, Emeritus Professor of Management, University of Manchester, has acted as my mentor, a role which has been crucial to the completion of this work.

I have greatly appreciated the assistance given by:-
the Chief Librarian, Manchester Central Library, and particularly the staff in the Local Studies and Archives departments. Also the Librarian and Archivist of Chetham's Library, Manchester.

The Dean and Chapter of Manchester Cathedral, in particular the Rev Canon Andrew Shanks (Canon Theologian), Lisa Greenhalgh (archivist); also Canon J Burns, the late Mr Philip Knowles, and Derrick Murdie, archivist of St. Mary's Church in Bowdon.

The Officers, Executive Committee and Volunteers of the Manchester and Lancashire Family History Society.

Those with connections to Bennett Street Sunday School have shared knowledge and photographs:
Marion and Bill Gow (the Bennett Street Charity);
Enid Cox, Mrs Ann Crouch (nee Cox),
Mrs Greta McElvogue (nee Fletcher),
Mrs Diana Parry (nee Timperley),
D Brian Cooper (David Stott's great-great grandson).

The following people have helped in a variety of ways:
Robert Bonner, Sheila Cathers, Julia Collinge, Chris Makepeace,
Mary O'Brien, Bevan Taylor, Brenda Wilson.
The late Brian Adshead of Romiley,
the late Brian Jepson of Crewe.

Special thanks must be given to those who have been connected in enabling the use of the work of L S Lowry; notably Claire Stewart, the curator of the Lowry Collection at The Lowry in Salford, Victoria Cole of DACS, the owner of *Going to School* and the Estate of L S Lowry who kindly gave permission for the oil to be used.

Finally, thanks too to Patricia Byron of Stellar Books.

Timeline

1801	Founding of Stott's school – attachment to St Paul's church
	Start of Manchester's Whit Monday walks
1811	Attachment to St Clement's
1818	Removal to Bennett Street – school thereafter named Bennett Street Sunday School
1819	Peterloo Massacre
1824	Re-attachment to St Paul's
1841	Start of the New Year parties
1843	Founding of the school's Literary and Educational Society
1843	Start of the day school
1847	Ten Hour Factory Act
1848	Death of the founder, David Stott
1861	Cotton famine
1870	Education Act
1871	Bank Holiday Act
1903	Day school transferred to Manchester Education Authority
1914-1918	The First World War
1919	Formation of the scout troop
1939-1945	The Second World War
1940	Closure of the day school
1950	L S Lowry paints an oil of the school façade.
1962	Winding up of the Literary and Educational Society
1966	Closure of the school

List of Illustrations

Every effort has been made to credit all the copyright holders of the photographs in this book, but where omissions have been made, the publisher will be glad to rectify them in any future editions.

Preface

As a child I attended Bennett Street Sunday School during its declining years. Even at such a young age I came to realise that it had a history, that in its prime it had been a significant and influential institution and its near empty rooms had once been filled to capacity with scholars like me – although *they* were learning to read and write.

The aim of this book is to bring the school back into the public eye and introduce its work to a new audience; to place on record its spiritual work, the humanity of its managers and the fact that not only did those scholars receive an education but they also found solace, companionship and enjoyment within its walls.

The administration was formalised during the early 1820s resulting in large, leather-bound minute books and it is in the copperplate script inscribed in these volumes, and the accompanying ephemera, that the later life of the school is revealed. As the founder apparently left no papers, the early history of the school has been taken largely from writings published internally for the school's centenary.

When it closed, Bennett Street Sunday School lodged its archive with Manchester Central Library and it is from these documents that this history has been written.

MWL

1

INTRODUCTION

The Sunday School Movement

St Paul's Bennett Street Sunday School was, in its heyday, an institution of considerable influence in the Manchester inner city area of New Cross. With up to 2,680 scholars on its books in the 1850s, it provided the children in its neighbourhood with a free primary education and secondary educational opportunities later leading to university study. Its many adult members too had access to wide-ranging learning experiences leading to all-round self improvement.

Where was Bennett Street?

If we look today at a modern street plan of Manchester we will look in vain for Bennett Street in New Cross and indeed for New Cross itself. Manchester street names were rationalised in the 1960s to achieve just one street per name. The Bennett Street which survived this exercise was adjacent to a large bus depot in the area of Gorton. The name of Bennett Street in New Cross was changed to Bendix Street and that is what we must look for.

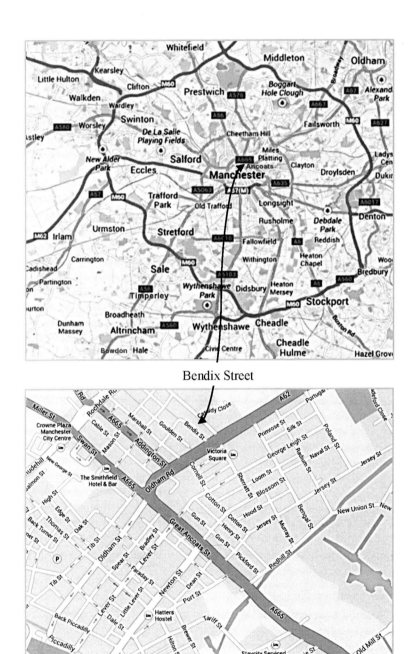

Bendix Street

Courtesy of Google Maps

If we trace our way from Piccadilly Gardens, up Oldham Street, straight across the Great Ancoats Street/Swan Street junction and continue up Oldham Road, we pass Cable Street and Addington Street on the left (between which two streets the 'new' church of St Paul's used to stand). A few yards further on, look on your left for Bendix Street and there, occupying the full block between that street and the next street (Thompson Street), just off the Oldham Road, stood Bennett Street Sunday School. For 150 years it stood there, not only a place of worship and a fount of education but also a centre for social life and a sanctuary for the people of its densely populated neighbourhood.

Always described as founded in 1801 by David Stott, the school (colloquially referred to simply as 'Bennett Street') owes its existence to the Sunday School Movement which spread rapidly through England in the late eighteenth century. Bennett Street, the largest Anglican Sunday school in Manchester, was sufficiently noteworthy to be mentioned in social history's wider literature[1]; one author awards it the accolade of being the 'greatest' Anglican Sunday school in the country.[2]

Social historians discuss the Sunday School Movement in the context of the French Revolution and this country's Industrial Revolution. The former brought about the overthrow of law and order, giving rise to the greatest atrocities; the latter saw the mechanisation of manufacturing, the migration of country dwellers to the towns, the shackling of the working-class in factories and the widespread use of child labour. There was little or no schooling for such children; they worked up to twelve hours a day for six days a week; on Sundays they ran riot in the streets causing disturbance and damage.[3]

It is generally accepted that the pioneer of the Sunday School Movement in the 1780s was Robert Raikes, a gentleman journalist and printer in Gloucester. Having seen children from his local factory running wild on Sundays he employed women to take them into their own homes to keep them off the streets and to teach them to read, specifically to read the Bible. From such small beginnings the Sunday School Movement grew. Sunday schools were established throughout the country by churches and chapels of varying denominations, by town committees and also by socialist organisations such as the Chartists and the co-operative movement. Philanthropic manufacturers opened them for their own employees, particularly in rural pockets of industrialisation, for instance at Styal, ten miles south of Manchester.[4]

In Manchester itself, a growing town with an increasing number of factories individually owned, a preliminary meeting with a view to organising Sunday schools was called in 1784. In 1788 they acknowledged they were witnessing 'a degree of profligacy and corruption of manners beyond the experience of former ages' and a public appeal was launched for assistance in addressing the problem: 'Every true friend to the interest of society, to peace and security will think himself obliged to promote the establishment of Sunday schools'. A 'Committee for Sunday Schools under the Establishment' (or the Church of England Schools Committee) was duly created and under its auspices Sunday schools were formed and attached to various churches. Bennett Street Sunday School metamorphosed out of one of these.[5]

Through the years Bennett Street Sunday School often referred to itself as 'unique'. Of course this was not so. Not only was the school a product of the Sunday School Movement but only six miles away, in Stockport, there was a non-denominational institution universally acknowledged as 'the largest Sunday School in the world'. Numerically Stockport was always at least twice as large as Bennett Street. And they were aware of Stockport's existence for in

1891 Stockport presented Bennett Street with a copy of Wild's *History of Stockport Sunday School* and Bennett Street reciprocated by sending a copy of their *Memorials* to Stockport.[6]

Where perhaps Bennett Street could be said to be more unusual than most was that, rather than being non-denominational or rooted in Methodism as many large Sunday schools were, Bennett Street was Anglican, speculating that

> 'I don't think there is another School in England exactly on the same footing...we are bound to be a Church of England School...but we may go to any church'.[7]

Only the consent of the relevant clergy was required.

The Sunday School Movement became a major influence on working-class life, the aims being to 'prevent vice, encourage industry and virtue [and] dispel ignorance'. For almost a century before state provision, they supplied religious instruction and reading and writing to children and illiterate adults on a Sunday, their only day free from their labour in the mills. Sunday school was simply school on a Sunday, and all with the underlying objective of calming the existing social tensions and improving the children's prospects.

The formation of the movement was however controversial. Certain philanthropists felt it advisable to remove children from the influence of their parents on a Sunday, a day which the adult poor were said to devote to sex, drink and gambling. Others saw such action as a threat to the liberty of the individual and there was a widespread view among a certain section of the labouring classes that Sunday schools were killjoys intent on depriving them of their Sunday pleasures.

Working-class aspirations to move 'above one's station' were most emphatically discouraged and therefore many of the new urban middle class did not approve of Sunday schools, considering that they made such a transition more likely. Would learning to read and write give children unsuitable social aspirations; would it deplete the pool of labour available to employers? Would marching the children to church in procession sow the seeds of a revolutionary militia? At this time when class consciousness was being clearly defined, many of the upper and middle classes were fearful that from such small beginnings a French-style revolution might take hold in Britain.

In the nineteenth century Sunday school attenders were invariably referred to as 'scholars' and originally tended to be the children of the destitute; by the mid-nineteenth century those attending were largely the children of the 'deserving poor', defined as those intent on acquiring respectability and perhaps just in need of advice and occasional short-term relief, or assistance in cash or kind, probably from their parish. New Cross housed a significant proportion of unemployed as well as those in part-time or casual work, and expenditure on alcohol was seen as the deciding factor between poverty and destitution. But not all members of the working-class were dissolute; there were those who, although poor, were hard working, temperate and as economically prudent as was possible. Many parents saw education and moral training as a way out of poverty and the route to a better way of life, but others saw the pitiful earnings of their children as the crucial factor between poverty and abject poverty.[8]

The original leaders of the Sunday School Movement were middle class. In Manchester the names of the organising committee of 1788 have come down through the years, philanthropists and wealthy business men such as James Kay, Samuel Greg, and Thos Philips; and others who have been perpetuated in street names, for instance Parker,

Mosley and Tipping. Many of the schools were started by local factory owners or members of the clergy and their working class scholars often rose through the ranks to positions of trust.

——————— * ———————

Throughout the country Sunday school leaders were initially agreed that Sunday was a day for religious instruction only, but soon found they had to use elementary secular texts to teach the reading. The teaching of writing was a much more controversial issue; it raged for decades. Some argued that in order to read the Bible it was not necessary to be able to write and therefore writing should not be taught on Sundays; others considered it an upper-class accomplishment; a factory workforce was not required to write. In Manchester the Church of England Schools Committee had prohibited writing classes on Sundays but permitted them on weekday evenings. In the 1840s only three Sunday schools (out of 86) in Manchester were teaching arithmetic; Bennett Street was one of these three.[9]

Sunday school education came to have a significant impact on working-class literacy but the movement did not concentrate its efforts solely on children. There were many illiterate adults and the national movement which developed in connection with education for working-class adults was the Mechanics' Institute (MI) movement. The foundation of the London MI in 1823 was closely followed by that of Manchester in 1824, an institution which Bennett Street sought to emulate. The aim of the MI movement was to instruct working men in the 'mechanical arts' and the principles of their trades. As the majority of Manchester's MI students were warehousemen and clerks rather than mechanics, bookkeeping, shorthand and commercial letter writing were added to the customary curriculum.[10]

The passing of the Ten Hour Factory Act in 1847 brought an increase in leisure time and the Sunday School Movement, always keen to promote abstinence and keep its members away from public houses, gradually provided a more social atmosphere. Also, towards the end of the nineteenth century the rise in commercial entertainment and sport prompted Sunday school leaders to provide such diversions on their own premises in order to retain the attendance of their older scholars. This provision, added to their internally organised welfare benefits, formed a 'total social package characteristic of the period', facilities that were 'not readily available elsewhere to the working-classes'. All these facilities were initiated by the voluntary philanthropic leaders who acted to supply the needs they saw in their own locality.[11]

Manchester as a whole recorded about 25,000 Sunday school children in 1849/50; Bennett Street alone had 2,611 scholars on its roll at that date. It was said that 'In no part of the town was such an institution more needed, and in none, certainly was it more successful'.[12]

2

1801-1818

The Early Years

St Paul's Bennett Street Sunday School, Manchester, was founded in 1801 by David Stott, and moved to its site in Bennett Street, New Cross, in 1818. Prior to that date it was known as Stott's School, a well-known institution operating from various smaller properties in the rapidly growing industrial area of Ancoats.

For the whole of the period the throne was occupied by George III; for most of the period the country was at war with France and/or Spain; the battles of Trafalgar and Waterloo took place in 1805 and 1815 respectively; and the slave trade was abolished in 1807. Beethoven was composing and Jane Austen was writing. In Manchester John Dalton published his work on atomic theory.

The districts of Ancoats and New Cross were situated half a mile or so from Manchester's centre and were divided by Oldham Road. In the nineteenth century Ancoats was an area of mills surrounded by poor, densely packed, housing. As an area, New Cross was considered perhaps slightly better than Ancoats and, rather than mills, contained warehouses, a large wholesale food market, and later railway sidings.

'At the period when the school came into prominence the lot of the poor was a very hard one. Times were bad, the hours of labour were terribly long and wages were low (in 1811 a weaver, when fully employed would earn but 11s[hillings] per week and a spinner 7s[hillings]). Bread and all the necessaries of life were exceedingly dear. Those were the days of riot and turnout, of incendiary fires, of the Luddites and the Blanketeers; and into the midst of that society came the Bennett Street School with unnumbered ministrations of help and consolation to those who needed them so much. At that time the school was the one bright spot in the lives of the people who lived around it'.[1]

By 1788 Manchester's General Committee for the Management and Support of Sunday Schools of the Established Church (the 'General Committee') had started to found Sunday schools, attaching them to various churches. The reports record that in 1794 Thomas Stott, the father of David Stott, was a teacher at a Sunday school in Newton Lane (later re-named Oldham Road) and that in 1804 father and son together taught (with two others) 851 scholars at a school in Gun Street Ancoats. Gun Street was one of four schools attached to St Paul's church in Turner Street. In 1805 two more small schools were added to St Paul's care, and David Stott progressed to greater responsibility; he was first master (of two) at the Primrose Street School where he had 350 scholars and five assistants. He was 26 years-old. Two years later there were 404 scholars; the school outgrew its premises and in 1808 Stott and his colleague had moved to larger rooms in an old and rickety building in George Leigh Street. They had 726 scholars and had become Manchester's largest Church of England Sunday school.[2]

All St Paul's schools had shown a modest increase in numbers but George Leigh Street, under the sole charge of David Stott, had almost doubled within twelve months from 804 scholars in 1809 to 1,526 in 1810; a testimony to the efficacy of David Stott's methods and an early indication of the care and friendliness his biographers were later to refer to. The number of assistants had also doubled, from twenty to forty. David Stott's influence was said to be 'extraordinary' in attracting and keeping teachers and scholars, and numbers continued to rise steadily at George Leigh Street until in 1814 there were 1,905 scholars. The rector recorded that in 1815 the total number of Sunday school scholars under the care of Manchester's General Committee was 8,000 and that about one quarter of those were supervised by David Stott.

Stott's School had become a household name in Ancoats as is illustrated by the following mothers' exchange which became one of the legends of the school.

"Eh, Mary, that's a rough lad o' thine. Aw doubt he'll come to no good".
"Ay, wench, he is, but what con aw do; his faither's dead an' th' lad's getten out of my reach".
"Well, tha should send him to 'Stott's Schoo',' they'd mak' some'at on him theer".[3]

There is plenty of evidence that David Stott did indeed 'make something' of the lads entrusted to his care, as well as evidence of their respect for the school and its leader.

Manchester's General Committee ran all its Sunday schools itself from the financial standpoint; it paid their expenses such as rent, and provided essential equipment, for instance in 1811 it ordered '300 Frames [to support the letters of the alphabet] for the Spelling sessions', but it took no part in their internal organisation, nor did it interfere. This method meant that the poorer districts such as Ancoats and New Cross benefited from money donated in the more wealthy areas. The internal organisation of the individual Sunday schools was in the hands of the relevant clergy and of Sunday school superintendents such as David Stott.[4]

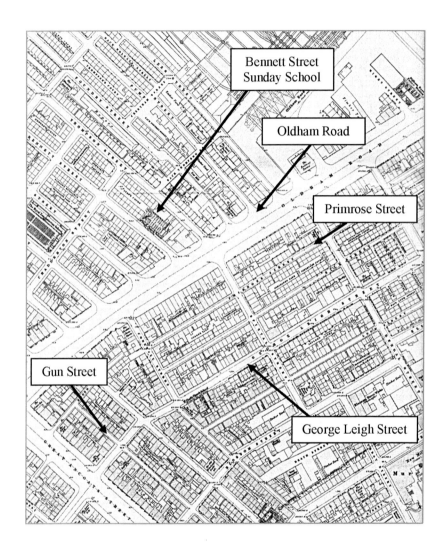

1849: Manchester New Cross and Ancoats, large scale plan a
yard to the mile, shows the early locations of Stott's School,
and the large Bennett Street Sunday School building.

(Copyright Alan Godfrey Maps – Manchester, sheet 24)

Many of the children attending Stott's School worked long hours in the surrounding mills, often from as young an age as five or six. School on a Sunday was therefore their only route to an education. David Stott taught his Sunday scholars to read and instructed them in 'the nature, the duties and the hopes of religion'. He encouraged loyalty to the King, coached them in morals, cleanliness and manners and marched them to St Paul's to attend service. It was during the Primrose Street days that, rather than simply attending church, he felt the children required religious instruction 'suitable to their tender years and untrained capacities'. Therefore, in about 1809, and in addition to its daytime operation, he opened his school on Sunday evenings and started religious improvement classes for scholars and the younger teachers. He read a sermon to them 'or something of that kind' and talked to them about it 'in a friendly way'. This approach was so successful that he extended these classes to a Tuesday evening also. By around 1814 there were 150 attending on Tuesday and 400-500 on Sunday.

Education

It was about 1809/1810 and because of the growth of the school, that David Stott saw the need for additional teachers. Contrary to the experience of many other Sunday schools, he found that in his area the required assistance was not forthcoming from 'the influential classes of society'. He therefore decided that the older scholars should be promoted to teacher status, but when the rolls had to be made out and the returns made for the General Committee, it was discovered that 'a serious obstruction lay in the way:- these young people could not write'. At that point he had around 1,500 scholars. David Stott acted promptly and started his 'Writing School', a weekday evening class. He then established further evening classes, teaching accounts and English grammar to those teachers and senior scholars who wished to learn. All tuition was free. Stott himself held the office of joiner and fitted and repaired the desks; he also made and mended the quill pens, 'metallic pens being scarcely known at that time'. Pens formed a large part of the expenses of the Writing School; four quarts of ink cost 2s 6d in 1816 and 100 bank pens 1s 9d; in 1823 pens were ordered in batches of 1,200. In 1815, following a visit to the school by Mr Thomas Robertson of Glasgow, a man much interested in Sunday schools, members of the Writing School used their lesson to write letters to a Sunday school in Glasgow. Those who were not sufficiently advanced to write their letters themselves dictated them to those who were, and the leaders collected the letters for posting.

In 1811 the allegiance of Stott's School was transferred from St Paul's to St Clement's in Stevenson Square. The details of this move will be covered at the point when the school returned to St Paul's in 1824, but it is necessary to mention it briefly here because of one occurrence which had a lasting impact.

It was the rector of St Clement's, Rev A Hepworth who, in 1813, introduced into Stott's School a young business man called Benjamin Braidley who, aged twenty-two, acted as a Visitor. Visitors were originally 'gentlemen who visited' Sunday schools out of philanthropic interest; their function was subsequently defined as being: 'chiefly consultative and advisory, especially in the case of delicacy or difficulty. They shall exercise a general supervision [including financial] over the school but not in such a way as to interfere.....with the Committee of Management'. The word 'Visitor' is given an upper case letter in order to differentiate one from a casual caller. Very soon Braidley became more active and began to play a leading role, jointly with David Stott. According to his diary for 1815, Braidley was present at the school all day on Sundays and on five evenings out of the remaining six. His weekly timetable was as follows:

'**Sunday**: (morning and afternoon) worship and reading classes;
(in the evening Stott and Braidley would explain a Bible chapter
to the scholars); at 8 pm after church 'there is a prayer meeting
until 9.15 or 9.30'.
Monday: the Writing School
Tuesday: meetings for prayer
Wednesday: writing and accompts;
Thursday: writing;
Friday: writing and accompts.
Saturday evenings: business meetings and candidates prepared
for confirmation.'

In 1815 Stott and Braidley divided the weekday religious classes, the
girls meeting on Tuesdays and the boys on Wednesdays. Braidley
confided that 'it does indeed give me great delight to hear the young
of both sexes rehearse their Christian experiences'. One girl had
'changed her employment and is placed among some giddy girls so
that she cannot enjoy her [...?] secret communion with God'. One of
the boys who had 'begun to be religious' questioned whether he and a
few companions had committed a sin by 'singing at people's doors on
Christmas morning'.[5]

The teaching of the scriptures by both Stott and Braidley was simple
and straightforward but achieved impressive results. The aim was
always to introduce the children to corporate worship in church and
the gradual increase of those attending communion services was noted
with satisfaction. Braidley stated that his personal aim was 'religious
instruction', his opinion being 'the mere art of teaching to read is of
questionable utility without this great aim'. And it was not only
children who were taught to read. His diary records his visit to Old
Catherine Prescott, often referred to as 'our old woman'. Aged 106 or
107 she had 'within the last three or four years' learned to read the

Bible. She had never before had the opportunity for, as she herself observed, 'there were none of these blessed Sunday Schools' in her day.

When his scholars had mastered the art of reading, David Stott wanted them to have access to books to read at home. At this period to own a few books was a luxury for most working-class people and, in spite of his reservations concerning reading, Braidley played an important part in raising £199 by subscription to set up a lending library within the school.

Prizes

It became tradition for the school to present books as prizes, or 'rewards' as they called them. Originally these were Bibles, prayer books and other religious books; later 'morally safe' fiction was also included. These rewards were initially for regular attendance but subsequently were also awarded, for example for 'proficiency in Biblical knowledge'. Financial contributions towards these books came from the teachers. The records of the reward books presented between the years of 1811 and 1813 indicate the size of the school. There were twenty classes of girls and nineteen of boys between the ages of four and twenty. Out of the first class (the older girls) twenty-six received a Bible or a Book of Common Prayer and a similar number of boys received either *Nelson's Devotions*, a Bible or a spelling book. The children aged between four and ten received spelling books 'of different sizes' or 'instructive tales'. No prizes were awarded until a scholar had attended for at least twelve months. According to Braidley, 1,635 books were given as rewards for regular attendance in 1815.

*

In the early nineteenth century districts such as Ancoats had an extraordinarily high rate of child mortality, largely attributed to the state of the housing and the sanitary conditions. One of the duties which Braidley undertook was visiting 'the cottages of sick and afflicted youth', and being present at the 'dying beds of the scholars and teachers'. It was not uncommon for adults connected to the school to have only one child, out of several, who survived them. Adults were dying chiefly in their fifties or earlier. Consumption was the most recorded cause of death of both adults and children; two out of the first three of Bennett Street's published *Memorials* record deaths from consumption in scholars aged between twelve and fifteen. Braidley visited 'with a view to do them some spiritual good' reading them portions of scripture to promote 'the peace and comfort of the afflicted soul'. He recorded his visits in minute detail.

When visiting Simon Taylor, Braidley 'found his dwelling to be of the humblest order, and its inhabitants of the humblest class of society'; Simon was aged 18 and had attended Stott's School since he was nine or ten; his father was dead; his mother described as 'industrious'. Simon Taylor had already been ill for eleven months when Braidley records:

'I saw that he would not continue long in this world...His mother informed me that when he was able to sit up, he was in the habit of reading some hymns out of book he had procured...I pointed out JESUS CHRIST to him as the sinner's only hope.'

On a second visit a few days later,

'After engaging in prayer I asked him whether he read much in the Bible. He replied that he was not able to sit up in bed so as to read much himself, but that his brother read for him...I found Simon was anxious to have the Bible read to him, and I promised to ask some of his schoolfellows to come and visit him for that purpose. I was glad to hear afterwards that they frequently did so'.

On a further visit,

'I here asked his mother for the Bible, and read the 6th chapter of St Matthew's Gospel...His mother seemed very thankful for my visit and said "Ay, sir, he likes you to come and see him; he has been talking about you all the day"'.

On subsequent visits Braidley introduced the Lord's Supper into his conversations and asked if Simon Taylor would like to receive communion.

'"If you wish it, I will speak to our worthy Clergyman on Sunday about it: and before I see you again, will you (if you should live) turn the matter over in your mind?" "Well, I will, sir; I think I should like to receive it."'

Visiting on the day Simon Taylor died, Braidley commented:

'I have seldom met with any who were more ignorant than he was when I first went to see him, and yet the all-powerful grace of God broke the stubbornness of his heart, and melted it into repentance'.[6]

Social Welfare

In addition to fostering spiritual welfare and providing elementary education, David Stott inaugurated a network of social welfare. To encourage thrift and foresight he started the school's own Sick Society in 1812; this was formed originally for teachers but in 1814 it was opened up to scholars aged fourteen and later to those over twelve years. Joining was optional but they had to be in good health to do so. The subscription was one penny per week. In cases of sickness the society paid out four shillings per week for six months, plus two shillings per week for 30 months more. With the parents deprived of a sick child's wages, this money would prove a welcome boost to the family income. At death, one more penny could be subscribed resulting in a benefit of an oak coffin plus five guineas in money. 'Our old Woman' mentioned above became the society's first pensioner. Braidley records that in 1815 'this being Christmas Day we had the Annual meeting [of the Sick Society]...and the children of their own accord voted the old woman four shillings a week during life'. She lived until 1817. David Stott also founded a Funeral Society for any of his scholars over five years of age. On payment of one penny only at the death of a member, the family became eligible for the same funeral allowance as that provided by the Sick Society.

Whit Week

Stott was also keen to introduce his scholars to fresh air and exercise and arranged outings for them; the records show that the attendance figures rose prior to those events! Manchester businesses took a holiday in Whit Week, the date of the early summer race meetings at nearby Kersal Moor[7]. Towards the end of the eighteenth century Manchester churches, unhappy at the juxtaposition of the race meeting and of Whit Sunday, a major festival of the Christian year, took action and began to organise their own Whit Week festivities in an effort to divert their members' attention from this rival attraction at Kersal. They considered attendance there to be immoral, an encouragement to indulge in drinking and betting and therefore likely to cause financial hardship among the working classes.[8]

Consequently a meeting of the General Committee was held at the Star Inn on 20 January 1801. It was resolved that 'all the children of the Sunday Schools of Manchester and Salford under the establishment be brought together to church on Whitsun Monday yearly to hear divine service' and that, church by church, they should parade from St Ann's Square to the Collegiate Church (now the Cathedral), walking 'six in a line, the girls first'. In 1811 the music for the procession was provided by the regimental band of the 2nd Royal North British Dragoons whose Colonel was thanked 'for his politeness in allowing them' to attend. The organisers were anxious that the occasion should be seen as a religious gathering rather than simply as a parade and the teachers were requested to suppress as much as possible 'gaudy and unbecoming dress'. This was the start of Manchester's Anglican Whit Walks of Witness which continued up to the twenty-first century. [9]

Originally this Whit Monday service had marked the anniversary of the founding of Sunday schools in Manchester, but by 1815 this latter celebration had been transferred to the Sunday after Ascension Day. On that occasion the town's Sunday school children were marshalled in designated areas (in the case of St Paul's and St Clement's this was Piccadilly), given a bun or cake and then shepherded back to their own churches where a sermon in support of all the Sunday schools was preached and a collection taken. [10]

The first time the Bennett Street archive mentions the Whit Monday Walk is in 1815. It proved to be a fateful day, Braidley recording in his diary that:

'Before the service [in the Collegiate Church] commenced I heard a dreadful scream or yell...the children all rose up in the greatest terror and such a scene of confusion and dismay ensued as it is impossible to describe.......it was discovered that the accidental breaking of a window was the first cause of the alarm, the children who were near it screamed which caused others to suppose that the Gallery was giving way…Their parents were flocking from all parts of the Town, having heard that the [Collegiate] Church had fallen in. After fruitless endeavours to pacify the children, it was thought advisable to send them home which was accordingly done and there was no service….One Boy was killed [belonging to Bennett Street] and five others are in the Infirmary but are likely to leave before the end of the week.'

Following this tragedy Braidley goes on to record the full week's events:

'**Whit Tuesday:** '[prayer] meeting was this Evening thronged';
Whit Wednesday: 'This day we took four-five hundred children to the Church when they were addressed by our worthy minister'… 'dined [along with several others] with Mr and Mrs Allen at their house and spent a pleasant evening'.
Whit Thursday: 'I went together with Mr Stott [and two others] and about 140 Teachers, Monitors and elder scholars to Blackley'. [They had dinner there with another Sunday school] and 'we afterwards went into the Earl of Wilton's Park where the children were much gratified'.
Whit Friday: 'Today we went to Chorlton and were about 160 in number where we attended Divine Service…and afterwards took tea upon a grass plot and then took a walk to the side of the River Mersey…When we came back we sang God Save the King'… 'both yesterday and today we sung many hymns in the open air which had a very fine effect'.

The school leaders were keen from these earliest times to introduce their scholars to open air activities, something which became tradition, and in the early nineteenth century they combined such outings with church worship.

To start the week in 1818, on Whit Sunday Benjamin Braidley took between 1,300 and 1,400 children to 'Wm T…'s grounds at Holt Town' (the south end of Ancoats) where 'the placid river Medlock was filled with fish [and] birdlife was seen on the banks' and that he 'treated them with a bun'. He also recorded that '800 came back to school and were electrified'. In those candle-lit days we imagine this to refer to the alternative dictionary definition of 'being greatly excited' or 'thrilled'.[11]

Social Activities

Christmas was another opportunity for social interaction and the first tea party was probably held in 1813; certainly the practice was established by 1815 when Braidley records that:

> 'This being Christmas Day…after the meeting [of the Sick Society] was over we treated all our teachers to tea who, together with a few strangers and the Old Woman amount to about 150. We spent the Evening in a pleasant and, I trust, a Christian manner'.

*

Because of the rapidly increasing numbers, Stott's School expanded to occupy premises in three separate buildings on both sides of George Leigh Street. Pressure on these buildings was severe for the school opened every night of the week, and during Sunday's hymn singing it was said that speech in the adjacent room could not be heard. The leaders were agreed that more robust and spacious premises were required and monetary collections towards this goal were started within the school in February 1815 with scholars and teachers promising amounts such as 2d, 3d or 6d each week. Prior to organising a public appeal for new premises, subscribers, 'magnates of the town' and other interested people were invited to visit George Leigh Street on Sunday afternoons to see for themselves the conditions in which the school functioned. Among those who accepted the invitation was Thomas Houldsworth, an MP and owner of one of the spinning mills in Ancoats. Houldsworth was brought to the school by one of its Visitors and was persuaded to ascend 'dark and perilous stairs' to a room where he saw an 'immense crowd of children', some of whom were probably from his own workforce. He pledged to give £50 towards a new building; the Visitor said 'That will not do; I am going to give that much myself'. 'Then', said Houldsworth, 'I will make it a hundred'.[12]

Interest in the project having been established, an appeal committee was set up and met twice in January 1818 at the Albion Hotel in Market Street; both David Stott and Benjamin Braidley attended. The first meeting considered the purchase of land and appointed twelve trustees; in addition to Houldsworth these included other local mill owners, Messrs Kennedy, Murray, and McConnel. At the second meeting a building committee (not including Stott and Braidley) was appointed with authority to purchase land and to 'proceed in the erection thereon of a proper building'. It was intended it should cater for 2,000-2,500 scholars. No further formal meeting took place until June when it was reported that land in Bennett Street had been leased for ninety-nine years at an annual rent of four pence per yard; the building committee was empowered to negotiate the 'sinking [of] a foundation…and [the] contracting for bricks etc. etc.'; they resolved to 'heat by flues'. Fundraising resulted in a subscription of one hundred guineas from the General Committee, and this was followed by others from the mill owners, Visitors, and from Stott and Braidley themselves. The figure raised was over £1,200. The parents were approached although 'the late distressed state of trade' was acknowledged; the teachers contributed about £400 and the scholars collected nearly £200. 'Other small subscriptions were procured in the town and the trustees advanced £500. In this way the total cost of the new building was obtained, being £2,524'.[13]

No further formal meetings were held until November when the committee met again, on this occasion in the school in George Leigh Street and a fortnight later, on 13 December 1818, the scholars walked in procession from George Leigh Street to take possession of their new building in Bennett Street.

Bennett Street Sunday School had been planned, built and fitted out in less than twelve months and this is the point at which a new chapter in the history of the school begins.

3

1818-1850

Bennett Street Sunday School

The first thirty years of the life of Stott's School, now settled in its new premises on Bennett Street, New Cross (and henceforth called the Bennett Street Sunday School, or simply 'Bennett Street') could broadly be described as a decade of reorganisation, followed by one of consolidation and one of advancement.

Nationally, George III remained on the throne until 1820 and was succeeded by George IV, William IV (1830) and Queen Victoria (1837); the period became an age of Free Trade, social reform at home and exploration overseas. Following the Reform Act of 1832 Manchester elected its first MPs, with the school's Benjamin Braidley (as Boroughreeve) taking the chair on nomination day. The penny post was inaugurated in 1840; the Repeal of the Corn Laws (1846) reduced the price of bread, and the Ten Hour Factory Act of 1847 limited working hours. The government made its first grants to schools. Charles Dickens and the Bronte sisters were among those writing; heavy stamp duty on newspapers put them out of the reach of the working class. It was the start of the age of the railway.

Between 1820 and 1830 the population of Manchester grew by over forty per cent. The Manchester Mechanics' Institute opened in 1824.

Manchester became a municipal borough in 1838, the first Free Trade Hall was built in 1840 and the Collegiate Church was re-designated a cathedral in 1847. Many immigrants escaping the Irish potato famine (1846-51) settled in the area. Some became scholars at Bennett Street and for many years afterwards the school collected for Sunday schools in Ireland. At this time the town also experienced a lengthy period of industrial unrest and Bennett Street, being situated on the edge of Ancoats felt this keenly as, following the end of the Napoleonic Wars, spinners were forced to accept wage reductions, a situation which led to serious industrial action in June 1818.

Stott's School moved into its new Bennett Street building in December 1818. On 16 August 1819 a massive, but peaceful, rally of workers and radicals campaigning for cheap bread and the vote, took place only about half a mile away on St Peter's Field. The crowd (estimated by some to be 30,000 and by others 150,000) was thought to be a danger to itself and to the town and its dispersal was ordered. Many were trampled on in the ensuing panic when the Manchester Yeomanry and the militia appeared wielding swords; fifteen died and over 600 were injured, many of them women and children. The event became known as the Peterloo Massacre. Later in the day:

'On the very evening of the 16th a mob attacked a shop in New Cross on the grounds that the proprietor was a special constable at St Peter's Field...There was sporadic violence in Manchester over the next few days particularly in the New Cross district...On the 17th a special constable was fatally injured there and on the 20th locals fought a pitched battle with the cavalry'.[1]

Members of Bennett Street Sunday School must have been in the front line of such events although there is no direct mention of it in the records and attendance fell only slightly, 1,625 being present on 22 August compared with 1,646 the previous Sunday.

That year *The Times* recorded the plight of spinners and weavers in New Cross as being 'heartrending and overpowering...streets confined and dirty...houses neglected and windows without glass'.[2] Crowds broke mill windows as near as Jersey Street in 1826 with similar problems continuing until the mid-1830s. The Plug Riots of 1842, when strikers halted mill production by pulling plugs from boilers, resulted in further protests against unemployment and high food prices. Bennett Street recorded that 'not a single individual connected with these schools is known to have taken any part whatever in the late disturbances in this town and neighbourhood'. The year of 1842 also saw the formation of Manchester's new police force which became an active presence in Ancoats and New Cross; formerly the militia had been sent for in times of trouble and disturbance. Stott's School's move into its new Bennett Street building was also a move from the district of Ancoats into the marginally better area of New Cross which, although described as one of the poorer parts of Manchester, was one where 'out of 157 [police] officers...no fewer than 85 lived'.[3]

In the 1820s the Bennett Street trustees built three cottages adjacent to the school to rent out; one cottage belonged to the rector. These properties were later improved with the addition of kitchens and the replacing of stone flagged parlour floors with boards. The school, along with other property owners in the street, made a start on its paving, for David Stott 'long before the fact was publicly or generally admitted' had voiced the opinion that unpaved streets were a cause of poor health. Even the main Oldham Road boasted only a certain amount of 'flagging for pedestrians'; the road itself was as yet unpaved. In 1830 the school asked the Surveyors of Highways to widen this flagging on the north-west side as in 'dirty weather' they were experiencing considerable inconvenience in walking the scholars to church.

The 1833 government inquiry into child labour provides insight into the lives of some Bennett Street scholars. A fine spinner's family consisting of husband, wife and five children had a combined income of about 25s a week; the rent of their house (four rooms, two on each floor) was 3s 6d a week and their diet was given as follows:

'*Breakfast* is generally porridge, bread and milk, lined with flour or oatmeal. On Sunday, a sup of tea and bread and butter. *Dinner*, on week days, potatoes and bacon, and bread, which is generally white. On a Sunday, a little flesh meat; no butter, egg or pudding. – *Tea time*, every day, tea and bread and butter; nothing extra on Sunday at tea. – *Supper*, oatmeal porridge and milk; sometimes potatoes and milk. Sunday, sometimes a little bread and cheese for supper; never have this on week days. Now and then buys eggs when they are as low as a halfpenny apiece, and fries them to bacon....They never taste any other vegetables than potatoes, never use any beer or spirits; now and then may take a gill of beer when ill, which costs a penny. Perhaps she and her husband may have two gills a week. Her husband never drinks any beer or spirits that she knows of beyond this....The furniture consists of two beds in the same room one for themselves, the other for the children; have four chairs, one table in the house, boxes to put clothes in, no chest of drawers, two pans and a tea-kettle for boiling, a gridiron and frying-pan, half-a-dozen large and small plates, four pair of knives and forks, several pewter spoons. They subscribe 1d a week for each child to a Funeral Society for the children. Two of the children go to school at 3d a week each; they are taught reading for this, but not writing. Have a few books, such as a Bible, hymn-book, and several small books that the children have got as prizes at the Sunday school. Four children go to Stott's Sunday school'.[4]

This particular family lived in conditions said to be 'somewhat under the average' for a cotton operative, but the 1848 street plan on page 12 shows the housing around the school to be mostly in closed courts or were 'back-to-back'; there were few 'through' terraced houses. Their water supply could have consisted of a water pump and there would have been one privy shared by perhaps up to twenty houses. Such home conditions contrast starkly with Bennett Street's instructions for the caretaker to clean 'the two water closets attached to the girls' rooms'.[5]

People living in such overcrowded and badly ventilated housing fell prey to diseases, the chief of which was pulmonary tuberculosis. Also, between 1832 and 1866 Manchester suffered four outbreaks of cholera. During the 1832 epidemic, although the Bennett Street area was not the most seriously affected, a temporary cholera hospital was set up on Swan Street on the route between school and church and was the scene of a riot when crowds stormed the hospital and carried patients back to their own homes. The cavalry was called in. Of the 443 patients treated there 234 died. This was the background to life at Bennett Street Sunday School in the first half of the nineteenth century.[6]

The jubilee of the Sunday School Movement fell in 1831 and was celebrated by Bennett Street on 8 September, William IV's coronation day. The Committee of Management provided 2,500 medals suspended on blue ribbon for the scholars, and when they discovered that the female teachers had agreed among themselves to 'go with ribbon of uniform colour in their bonnets', they recommended that the male teachers should sport blue and red rosettes in their coats.

Throughout the 1830s and 1840s successive Factory Acts limited the hours of child labour and introduced part-time weekday schooling. Even so Bennett Street's rooms were occupied almost every evening: 'five nights out of six' is commonly referred to. The new building had been built to house 2,000-2,500 scholars and on the first occasion attendance reached 2,000, the whole school was paraded outside in front of David Stott to commemorate the fact.

The Building

Bennett Street Sunday School remained attached to St Paul's church on Turner Street although it was now situated in St George's parish. Contemporary pictorial evidence of the school is sparse, just etchings of one façade. Towards the end of the school's life, in 1950, L S Lowry painted an oil of the façade entitled *'Going to School'*.[6a]

There is one undated architectural plan of the school and also plans of the proposed alterations of 1900. No illustrations of the interior seem to survive and the following description has been compiled from references in the centenary history and from oral evidence.

Even its most loyal members never described the Bennett Street building as handsome; the words used were 'dismal', or at best 'factory-like'. It was later confessed that at the time of planning there had been no idea of public architecture, mills and churches being virtually the only large structures in the town. The school was based on the model of a mill 'four storeys high and enough room for mules and jennies' but in spite of this it was considered 'wisely arranged for its purpose' of catering for 2,000 scholars. It dominated the neighbouring cottage property. Originally the interior was whitewashed and heated by a fire stove. Each floor consisted of one large room (60ft x 40ft) plus a few ante-rooms. The windows were set high in the walls with no sills on which children could climb, although each large room had a central row of supporting pillars which seemed just made for them to swing around. Ventilation was always a problem and over the years many adjustments were made; one method was to replace some glass with louvred windows to provide a permanent flow of air.[7] The rooms were identified by number: No 1 room (ground floor) housed the younger boys; No. 2 room on the first floor was used by the older boys; No. 3 room (second floor) was for the younger girls and No. 4 room on the third floor was the home of the older girls and the ladies. Each room was under the control of an appointed manager and had its own harmonium and a free-standing pulpit, referred to as 'the desk'. This arrangement continued until after the Second World War. The undated plan shows that the ground floor at one time was (or it was proposed that it should be) divided into two school rooms, one smaller classroom and a library.

Early applications from members for the extra use of rooms, for instance to use 'No. 2 small room' for extra reading practice, were usually agreed subject to the applicant providing the necessary 'candles and coals'. This meant bringing their own candle and 'remunerat[ing] the porter for his trouble in making the fires'. In 1832 arrangements were under way for gas pipes and burners to be installed for lighting No 2, No 4 and all the small rooms; the leaders of the writing school gave £10 towards the expense. Writing in 1880 the rector recalled that:

> 'more than 40 years ago [the attempt to install gas lighting had been made] with portable oil gas, but both the attempt and the company that supplied the material were failures and candles were still used in the Bennett Street Night School for some years after. This portable gas was carried about in black cylinders, about two feet six inches long and eight inches in diameter'.[8]

The school premises extended for the complete width of the block between Bennett Street and Thompson Street. There were separate entrances for girls and boys, each with the necessary boot scraper; and in addition the girls were required to leave their pattens (platform soles strapped to boots to keep them out of the mud) at the bottom of the stairs. There was a yard on the Thompson Street side which was the site of the earth closets. Thompson Street at that time was a narrow street of similar width to Bennett Street rather than the main thoroughfare which it became in the twentieth century. This building was the centre of Bennett Street Sunday School's work for the next 150 years.

Attachment to St Clement's Church: 1811-1824

From its foundation Stott's School had been attached to St Paul's but when members of Manchester's General Committee inspected each church district in 1811, they were asked to decide 'which of the schools in St Paul's District shall hereafter be attached to St Clement's Church' (on the corner of Stevenson Square and Lever Street). At this point, while still occupying its premises in George Leigh Street, Stott's School was allied to St Clement's church.[9]

Bennett Street however remained a self-governing institution. It owned its own building, raised its own funds, planned its own services and duties and provided the personnel to carry them out. It was a charity run by the laiety, by philanthropists.

It was during this time that an etching was drawn of the school's façade. As the school's full title was (with the exception of this brief intervention) St Paul's Bennett Street Sunday School, this etching has often been a cause of confusion.

The first six years of the new attachment seem to have passed without comment until, in 1817, a new rector was appointed to St Clement's. Rev William Nunn was a man with a background of work in Sunday schools of a more conventional pattern, and in addition to promoting

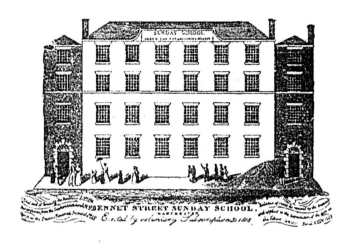

Above: Etching of St Paul's Bennett Street Sunday School

Below: Etching of the school as printed during the affiliation to St Clement's Church

(Bennett Street Memorials)

the gospel within Stott's School he sought to regularise both the teaching there and the conduct of the teachers. He attended the school on Sundays; he chaired committees; he immersed himself in the school's work. Such all-encompassing activity was seen by the trustees and Visitors as interference. Nunn's outlook was described as evangelical and Calvinistic, and his efforts to impose his type of teaching may have been the root of the controversy which developed. The school's methods, following David Stott's example of promoting 'freedom of action' and 'considerable breadth of view', had always been seen as successful, certainly from the point of view of scholar numbers.

With such polarised opinions on display, the relationship between the Bennett Street Committee and the rector became increasingly acrimonious and it was Benjamin Braidley, in his capacity as secretary to the school's trustees, who brought the matter to a head. While acknowledging in letters to Nunn in June and July 1824 that he was industrious and zealous, he claimed that Nunn was 'preaching doctrines contrary to the Church of England'. But there were also personal problems between this minister and the school leaders. Braidley accused Nunn of 'acknowledg[ing] none from the School to be [of] religious character' except those who attended his Friday night meeting; but perhaps crucially he also asked Nunn to explain his 'partially setting aside the Superintendence of Mr Stott'. At a Special Meeting of the Executive of Manchester's General Committee in July 1824 it was finally decided that:

'in consequence of irreconcilable differences now existing between a majority of the Visitors of Bennett Street Sunday School and Nunn and of the great desire generally expressed by the trustees, visitors and teachers that the school should be separated from St Clement's Church'.

The school was re-attached to St Paul's and never strayed again.[10]

Administration

Between 1822 and 1824 under the chairmanship of Rev Nunn with his 'business-like mode of procedures', the Visitors' and Teachers' Meeting had amended the rules and issued a formal 'Plan' (or timetable) for the Sunday sessions and this continued for some years.

This is a copy of the form for the Direction of the Superintendents – for the Upper Rooms of Boys or Girls – for the week they did not attend church. Numbers were too great for all to attend church together and a rota system operated. At this point males and females attended on alternate weeks.

Morning

H M		M
9.05	Preparatory Advice, Deliver Hymn Books. Hymn.	15
9.20	Call the (Teachers' and Scholars') Rolls.	5
9.25	Hymn and Prayer.	15
9.40	Collect Hymn Bks. Deliver Spelling Bks. Appoint lessons, Study.	15
9.55	Collect spelling bks. Form divisions. Teach.	10
10.05	Change divisions.	10
10.15	Join divisions. Improve lessons.	10
10.25	Sit down, give out notices, Call the 2nd Roll, write notices after absentees.	10
10.35	Give out reading bks. Appoint and Study lessons.	15
10.50	A hymn, Form divisions, Teach.	15
11.05	Change divisions.	10
11.15	Join divisions, Improve lessons.	10
11.25	Sit down. Collect Books.	5
11.30	Form divisions, Teach Catechism.	10
11.40	The Admonition, and hymn.	10
11.50	Collect hymn bks, Deliver hats or bonnets. Dismiss.	

Afternoon

Time	Activity	Min
1.25	Preparatory Advice. Deliver hymn bks. Hymn.	15
1.40	Call the (Teachers' and Scholars') Rolls.	5
1.45	Collect hymn bks. Deliver spelling bks. Appoint lessons. Study.	15
2.00	Collect spelling bks, Form divisions, Teach.	10
2.10	Change divisions.	10
2.20	Join divisions. Improve lessons.	10
2.30	Call the 2nd roll. Make collections.	10
2.40	Give out reading bks. Appoint and study lessons.	15
2.55	A Hymn, Form divisions, Teach.	15
3.10	Change divisions.	10
3.20	Join divisions. Improve lessons.	10
3.30	Sit down, Collect Books.	5
3.25	The Admonition and Religious instruction.	15
3.50	Hymn and Prayer.	10
4.00	Collect hymn bks. Deliver hats or bonnets. Dismiss'.	

The pattern varied slightly for the classes that were due to attend church that day. For them, psalters were distributed at 9.40am and their teachers would lead them through the church service, teach them the congregational responses and help them to find the appropriate places in their psalters. The timetable for the lower rooms was similar except that when the spelling books were collected, the younger scholars then had a session where they 'spell[ed] from memory'.[11]

In 1827, when re-attached to St Paul's, a new committee structure was established. The trustees (Messrs Stott, Braidley and Priestley) resolved to hold more regular meetings and to appoint some of the Visitors to help them. This new body was 'the Committee of Management' (sometimes referred to simply as 'the committee'). The

Committee of Management ran the school up to closure, its membership gradually evolving into secretary, treasurer, room managers, (or 'conductors' as they were called in the early days), Visitors and representatives of the trustees (and much later representatives of the teachers). The rector of St Paul's was normally invited to take the chair. He presided and spoke on Founder's Day and other celebrations and prepared candidates for confirmation, but there is no evidence that he was involved in the weekly running of the school.

OLD CHURCH OF ST. PAUL,
Consecrated 1765.

Above: The old church of St Paul on Turner Street

(Bennett Street Memorials)

The Rules

By the 1830s it was widely accepted throughout the country that there was a considerable difference between the behaviour of Sunday school children generally and those who did not attend; this was attributed to the necessary adherence to rules, the aim being to ensure quiet and orderly behaviour. Bennett Street rules, which were read out quarterly in each room, were not directed solely at scholars but also at teachers (who were mostly from the working class), superintendents and even Visitors who were 'most respectfully solicited' not to deviate from the plan. Emphasis was placed on cleanliness, appropriate behaviour, attendance and time-keeping for all. Superintendents were required to be on the premises five minutes before the opening of the sessions, to pay strict attention to the plan and not to leave their rooms without arranging appropriate cover.

Teachers' rules covered their conduct and time-keeping; in addition to teaching they were to maintain order and to obey the room superintendent. At this point there were over 100 teachers (the youngest of whom might be only 16 years of age); they were paid a small wage (in 1823 it was proposed that this should be raised to 6s 6d per quarter); if late they were fined 2½d and if absent 5d per half day. These fines were put towards the children's prizes.

Scholars' rules defined the starting age as four and required that they should be respectful and obedient to their teachers and not run about; fruit or playthings were not permitted. On first entering their room all scholars and teachers were required to observe a moment of silent prayer:

'Oh Lord, grant Thy blessing on the instruction given in this place. Give me I pray Thee, the hearing ear and the understanding heart. Grant me grace to know and do Thy will both now and evermore. Amen'.

Only one child at a time was allowed to leave the room to 'go into the yard' and scholars could not go home before time without leave. Although not a specific rule, it was suggested that any scholar meeting the minister or a leader in the street should give some token of respect 'such as a bow or a curtsey'.

The Bennett Street leaders rigorously enforced discipline. Any transgressions by teachers or scholars were severely dealt with. In 1828 two scholars who 'wantonly broke the School windows' had their names recorded and were made to pay for the damage. This approach however was not totally successful as, although one scholar came forward and paid, the other did not, 'and cannot be found'. Again, in 1833 scholars causing a disturbance were warned that, should it occur again, a constable would be sent for and the culprits taken into custody. In 1847 the leaders were called upon to deal with an incident considered sufficiently serious to warrant expulsion. The not insubstantial sum of 8s 11½d was found to be missing; the culprit was brought before the committee chaired by David Stott, but 'out of consideration for the delicate state of health in which his Mother has been, and continues likely to be, the Committee agreed to continue him in School for the present'. There was no compulsion to attend Sunday school but those who did so should obey the rules.

Anniversary Sunday

Bennett Street's anniversary Sunday with its attendant monetary collection was instituted in 1824 at a point when Manchester churches were beginning to sever their links with the General Committee.

Individual churches, including St Paul's, were preferring to retain their money for their own needs rather than paying it into the General Committee's fund. This fund had paid the rent of Bennett Street's building along with its annual expenses and, although the congregation of St Paul's had always shown 'great liberality' in their support of Bennett Street, the change made it necessary for the school to seek additional funds. From this time onwards the annual anniversary collection became the main source of income and anniversary Sunday one of the high spots of the school's year. The first collection took place in 1824 and 'it is believed' amounted to £12; thereafter it rose steadily. Anniversary Sunday was celebrated on the third Sunday in Advent, mid-December, and marked the anniversary of the day the school transferred from George Leigh Street to Bennett Street.

Religion

Having formalised the administration, the Visitors and Teachers' Meeting (and its successor the Committee of Management) turned its attention to assessing both the religious and the secular teaching. During the 1820s St Paul's did not hold Sunday evening services and so, following their re-attachment there, Bennett Street extended their own Sunday evening meeting. This was considered to be a successful means of 'communicating much spiritual benefit' and for many years attendance numbered between 400 and 500. In 1831 the school numbered 'nearly one hundred Church communicants' from its ranks. One rather prosaic result was that Bibles and other books wore out more quickly, and in 1827 application to the Society for Promoting Christian Knowledge resulted in the receipt of 'ten pounds in Bibles and Testaments'. The school provided sufficient books for each child to have sole use of a Bible and a dictionary for the spelling classes, but hymn books were shared; psalters and catechisms were even fewer.

Before a scholar could move from the lower room to the upper, they had to prove they could repeat the Creed, the Lord's Prayer and the Ten Commandments.

Scholars' church attendance was changed from males and females attending on alternate weeks to half of each room being taken each week: the first indication of mixed sex classes on Sundays. The procession between school and church was re-organized so that the youngest walked first. Previously 'the older children have proceeded first and walking much quicker than the youngsters, the latter have been left behind or kept running after'. It was also the intention to achieve an orderly exodus from church after the service so that the remainder of the congregation was not disturbed by them 'rushing out of church...particularly the boys'.

The school used 'Hymns for the use of Sunday Schools in Manchester', a small book (approximately 6x4x½ inches) published in 1839. The hymns were divided into the church seasons and those of nature; they included hymns which are still in use in the 21st century; among those which have not survived were 'Let dogs delight to bark and bite for God has made them so'. The prayers included one specifically for Sunday schools based on the Ten Commandments and enumerated all those connected with the movement, '...may we the several members of this charity work together with one another...for the good of the whole...visitors...clergy... parents...teachers...scholars...'.

As a further means of spreading the gospel a school Tract Association was formed in 1825, and in 1831 Benjamin Braidley reported that in those six years 'upwards of *ninety thousand* (his italics) religious tracts have been dispersed among the scholars at the expense of the teachers'. Tracts were considered an appropriate method of encouraging regular attendance and 'securing the affections of the children'. There was also a Bible Association through which teachers, scholars and parents could purchase Bibles at reduced prices.

It was generally acknowledged that the teachers were the lynch pin of the Sunday School Movement and during this period a fundamental change in their status took place. In 1830 the Committee of Management noted that 'in every school in the town consisting of 300 children except our own, the system of gratuitous instruction is operating' and quite soon afterwards a proposal to discontinue the payment of teachers was carried. Instead of payment, from 1831, teachers received an annual book prize of their own choice inscribed: 'Presented by the Visitors to…as a token of their approbation of service rendered as a gratuitous Teacher during the past year'. This custom remained up to the Second World War.

In 1847 the teachers were meeting each week and, led by clergy or a Visitor, were helped to prepare their lesson for the following Sunday. Of the 120 teachers on the roll at this time, 112 had been promoted from the ranks of scholars. It was said that an average attachment to a Sunday school in Manchester was four years, whereas around 1830 at Bennett Street, because of the influence of David Stott it was six years. The step from scholar to teacher could be large. Not only did the new teacher assume a certain authority and responsibility but they were also expected to contribute financially, for instance towards religious tracts, prizes and buns. The committee was concerned as to whether in times of unemployment the teachers (particularly the young ones) could manage such contributions and the phrase 'if they can afford it' is added to more than one resolution.

There is no evidence that Bennett Street had its own choir as many Sunday schools of the period did, and music found favour only spasmodically. In 1833 it was decided that one of the rooms was 'now not to be used for singing on weekday evenings…its moral effect having been in our opinion very injurious', but in the 1840s lectures on Psalmody were being given by a professor of vocal music from Kings College, London.

Innovations during the 1820s and 1830s were often the result of requests from teachers or older scholars. Self-help was always encouraged. Formal requests were made for a week-day class in religious instruction and for the establishment of a temperance society; one teacher asked for the use of a room to 'improve himself and others in reading', another requested permission to teach singing. All such requests were granted on the usual condition regarding coals and candles.

Education

The reading classes were divided into alphabet, one syllable and two syllable classes and by 1831 250 of the 'oldest and most deserving scholars' were also being taught writing and 'accompts' on two evenings per week; 'they find their own copybooks and candles but are at no further expense'. With the growth of the writing school pens continued to be a major expense with the school purchasing between 1,200 and 1,700 quills per annum. In 1839 when 170 males and 96 females were learning, the writing school had reached such a size that rather than attempting to continue mending pens themselves, this task became a charge on the committee, the Visitors voting to double their own subscriptions to absorb this extra expense. During this period the salaries for three masters teaching for two nights in each of the Writing School, the Arithmetic School and the Grammar School were also reviewed.

Part of the adult education movement in the nineteenth century was the nation-wide establishment of mechanics institutes, voluntary associations intended to promote self-improvement among the working classes. In 1839 adult education was addressed at Bennett Street. The leaders considered it important that the young should be given the opportunity to extend their knowledge beyond the stage of elementary reading, writing and arithmetic and so 'what would best be described as a Mechanics' Institute' was formed, offering 'most of the elementary subjects as well as vocal music, drawing and mathematics'; lectures were delivered and a reading room opened. But this mechanics' institute was short-lived. Only four years later, in 1843, we find that 'the Mechanics' Institute having ceased to exist, a Mutual Improvement Class is begun'. This latter group became a great success and developed into the Literary and Educational Society (always known colloquially as 'the Lit'). It remained in continuous existence for 120 years.[12]

Bennett Street Day School

From 1843 the leaders also ran a totally separate day school on the same premises which is briefly covered in Chapter 9, page 155.

Prizes

The leaders continued to encourage reading for pleasure. In 1825 1,561 books were given as prizes. Books of divine songs, psalters and copies of *Nunn's Hymns* had been given in the early years of the period but after the Visitors expressed a wish to make the prizes both interesting and informative, titles such as *Young Woman's Monitor, Mrs Trimmen's Rural Economist, Whole Duty of Man* and *Bunyan Explained* were presented.

By 1831 the Lending Library, established in the George Leigh Street days, boasted 650 volumes. In addition to adults, membership could include scholars providing they were recommended by a teacher or a Visitor; the charge was 6d (for the rules) and 2d per month thereafter 'towards keeping the books in repair'.

Welfare and Charity

The welfare network flourished. By 1831 the membership of the Sick and Funeral Society numbered 1,930 at a time when there were 2,700 scholars on the roll and around 80-100 teachers and leaders. Since its foundation in 1812 this society had helped 2,166 sickness benefit cases and assisted with 140 funerals.

The culture of charitable giving was similarly maintained and 'each year a very large sum is raised for various public and private charities and associations'. However during this period of what was termed financial 'distress', the school found that it was itself receiving charitable help. In 1827 a Manchester Ladies' Bazaar gave them 440 articles of clothing and thirty-three pairs of clogs which were distributed to scholars 'who are in want'. In the 1840s David Stott received £5 from the Mayor's Town Hall Charity and this he shared out between ten individuals.

Whit Week

By the 1820s the Whit Monday procession to service in the Collegiate Church was firmly established; in 1830 the seating plan shows space for 240 Bennett Street boys in the choir area and an allocation for 290 girls on the north aisle of the nave.[13] Following the Walk there was a Monday afternoon trip for teachers and older scholars. Wednesday and Thursday afternoons were reserved for scholars' sports days when the children marched to nearby farmers' fields where they took part in games and races; free buns or currant bread were provided. In 1830 1,500 buns were ordered for one of these outings, the caretaker opening the school doors at 5am to take delivery. In the same year 300 quarts of buttermilk were bought individually by the children from the farmer. On the Friday there was an all-day outing for teachers, adults and older scholars. The Manchester to Liverpool Railway opened in 1830 and soon afterwards railway trips became the norm, the teachers being required 'to assemble in the morning at 6.30 to go by the railway carriages to Liverpool'.

Social Activities

Social activities continued and expanded, the Christmas day tea party for the teachers having become tradition:

> 'in the old days before the era of boilers and tea-urns had arrived, a kind of camp-fire was made in the school-yard, and the old wives lent their copper kettles to boil the water, and their treasured crockery to supply the tables for tea'.

At Christmas 1833, a Georgian silver tea service with the following inscription was presented to David Stott:

> 'This Teapot with Sugar Bason [sic] and Cream Jug was presented to Mr David Stott, by the Visitors, Superintendents and Teachers of the Bennett Street Sunday School, Manchester, as a mark of the high esteem they entertain of his long and valuable services. December 25th 1833'.[14]

The New Year parties started in 1841; there were two, one on New Year's Eve and a second on New Year's Day; both included tea and entertainment but the price for New Year's Day was always higher. The New Year parties were for everyone and were 'very popular among the children'; three large rooms holding 1,200-1,500 'have frequently been filled'. The various classes organised 'tea drinking' parties for their own members at other times of the year; an (un-named) party enjoyed a round of beef and three hams in June 1838.

*

In 1845 the deaths of several of the original trustees were reported. Rather than the local industrial giants of the past the new trustees were drawn from the fields of commerce and retail: there was one surgeon, three merchants, two agents and a draper. They were mostly Bennett Street men whose names were to re-echo down the years, sometimes for generations. Rather than widening the circle at executive level, the school continued to recruit from within, a method which had been forced upon them in their earliest days of teacher shortage.

Benjamin Braidley died in 1845 aged 52 and, although he had been such a prominent presence in Manchester itself as well as in the life of the school, his funeral took place privately in his home town of Sedgefield in County Durham. Following Braidley's death the school obtained a copy of his portrait and asked David Stott to sit for his.

Stott and Braidley had alternated as chairman of the Committee of Management; after this date Stott took the chair, his last attendance being 8 February 1848. At the next meeting, 26 February, his death was reported. He was 68-years-old. Honouring their founder, Bennett Street members played a full part in his funeral at Bowdon church, their large presence being said to be 'quite unprecedented'. At the school's expense conveyances for the Visitors and superintendents were provided; they hired a band, prepared an obituary and ordered '200 mourning labels for the inside of the Teachers' hats'. The school erected an obelisk over David Stott's grave inscribed with a short eulogy. Subsequently and until the school closed in 1966, a representative of the trustees visited it each year to check that it was in good repair. After the closure a sum of money was left to ensure that the grave continued to be maintained.[15]

In the space of three years Bennett Street lost both its founder and the man who had worked so closely with him. All the evidence is that Stott never sought the limelight and that he left no writings. The school in which he had invested so much time, effort and forethought had developed from a personal educational charity into a firmly based committee-run institution. It had become the largest Sunday school in the borough and it did not falter in continuing to work to his ideals.

DAVID STOTT, 1779 – 1848

That David Stott was known as the founder of Bennett Street Sunday School was a mark of the utmost respect and affection. Because of the lack of early records generally and the fact that he left no writings of his own, it is difficult to be precise on the subject of the foundation. Opinion among the writers of the nineteenth and early twentieth centuries was divided. Some accounts state that the school was founded under the auspices of the Manchester General Committee for the Sunday School Movement and others that Bennett Street 'was really founded by David Stott'. Whatever the circumstances in 1801, the transfer of Stott's School from George Leigh Street to Bennett Street in 1818, was most certainly the work of David Stott; 'he selected the site, drew the plans, superintended the erection and lived to see the building out of debt'.

Bennett Street Memorials published in 1880 depict a man whose very nature fitted him for Sunday School work; unostentatious and unassuming in manner, he was judicious, a man of simplicity and affection who devoted all his days to Bennett Street. He did not discuss the 'abstract theory of Sunday Schools' preferring to exert a 'simple and firm determination... to try what could be done to benefit the neglected youth of our country'. No matter how poor or how ill-clothed, the children of the area found in David Stott a helper and a friend; on market days he filled his pockets with fruit to brighten their lives. One of his colleagues observed that Stott never excelled at what was understood as eloquence but had 'the high art of making his conversational addresses interesting'. His main objective was that the young people should be given the greatest possible advantage in life.

Years later his early scholars spoke of the fatherly affection David Stott had always shown in keeping a kindly watch over them. It was thought that this family bond and home-like sympathy was a 'sacred heirloom' which came to mark out the character of the Bennett Street School. What but this family bond, they asked, accounted for the fact that so many of those who moved away felt impelled to maintain their connection and that, together with those who remained, they continued to support the school with 'unprecedented zeal and liberality'. It seems that the feelings of 'family' never diminished; the records of 1966 state that a great-grand-daughter of David Stott's was present at the closing service. Such was his legacy: everything which followed was built upon what had been originally planned and executed by him and followed through under his influence and presence.

David Stott was born in Ripponden in West Yorkshire on 10 September 1779, the son of Thomas Stott a farmer and woollen manufacturer. He was eleven when the family moved to Manchester, a period when the cotton trade was beginning to develop. His father joined the firm of Thomas Houldsworth, a cotton mill in Ancoats and this firm displayed great interest and gave generous support to Bennett Street to the end of the school's life. Thomas Stott was in charge of the mule spinning department, a post which required him to visit the homes of the outworkers. By so doing he saw at first-hand the poor conditions in which these workers and their families lived. He was moved to open a Sunday school for such children in Gun Street and this was where his son David became a scholar.

As a boy David Stott was no model child; he behaved as boys do; he was a rough looking lad who loved playing with whipping tops and marbles and, against the rules, sometimes took these playthings into Sunday school. On one such occasion he was commanded to empty his pockets and place the contents on the fire shovel; authority, in the person of his father, then punished him before the whole school. It may be that these early experiences had a bearing on his later rapport with his own young scholars.

After attending Manchester Grammar School for three years Stott started work in the city as a warehouseman at Worthington's, a silk manufacturer. He stayed with the company for forty-five years becoming their leading manager and confidential adviser. He travelled to London by stagecoach buying goods and paying cash on the spot, and when the company branched out into making umbrellas he journeyed to Spain to purchase cane for the frames. He was incorruptible; nothing would induce him to accept a gift or a gratuity. In appearance he was 'like a well-to-do working man'... rather below the middle height, modest and undemonstrative, careful and solicitous'. He married in 1802 and had four children. His leisure time was devoted to reading and he was heard to say that the longer he lived the more he learned to respect the religious and political views of others. Through his influence this breadth of opinion became a distinguishing feature at Bennett Street.

It is evident that in many ways David Stott was quietly ahead of his time, specifically in recognising the needs of poor children in the fields of health, education, moral and religious training and welfare provision. He worked in the school until the last week of his life and died in February 1848 aged sixty-eight years. The feelings of respect and affection so apparent during David Stott's lifetime did not diminish after his death and Bennett Street erected a monument over his grave.

The inscription on the gravestone reads:

'SACRED to the memory of DAVID STOTT the FOUNDER
of ST PAUL'S SUNDAY SCHOOL, BENNETT STREET,
MANCHESTER WHO DIED FEBRUARY 26th 1848
AGED 68 YEARS.
"For to me to live is Christ and to die is gain"
He founded this Institution in the Year 1801 and was
permitted by the goodness of God to labor in the
Management of it until the last week of his life.
His Gentleness and Devotion aptly fitted him for a
SUNDAY SCHOOL Instructor. His Benevolence and
Discretion enabled him to foster this Institution equally
Eminent for its Usefulness and Success.
He was also the Originator of Sick and Burial Societies in
connexion with SUNDAY SCHOOLS and was a noble
Example of what may be effected by the Influence of
Christian Principle, Affection and Perseverance when
devoted to the service of the SAVIOUR
This tribute of Affection is erected in Veneration of his efforts
and Example by the VISITORS, Teachers and Friends of the
said SCHOOL'.

Also interred in the grave is 'JANE HIS WIFE WHO DIED
MAY 11th 1851 AGED 70 years'.

.

DAVID STOTT.

BENJAMIN BRAIDLEY.

(Taken from Bennett Street Memorials)

BENJAMIN BRAIDLEY: 1792 – 1845

Benjamin Braidley was introduced to Stott's School by Rev A Hepworth his parish rector in 1813. He was twenty-two and 'He seems… scarcely to have entered before he began taking a leading part in its affairs'; for the next ten years his work there dominated his leisure time. It is recorded that 'in the early history of that School his exertions and his influence stand out'. He trained the monitors and teachers and was superintendent of the Older [Upper] Boys Room at a time when this numbered 500 scholars His rebukes were considered 'judicious and successful' and a gentle 'hush' from him was often sufficient to obtain almost perfect stillness'. While not 'love[ing] him as a father' as they did David Stott, they did 'respect[ing] him as a friend'.

He was said to have 'a sincere and single faith in the power of God's word' and taught the scriptures with simplicity. In 1815 Rev Hepworth suggested that he train for the ministry. Braidley decided against this proposal but his diaries record that he was in the school all day on Sundays, including the evening scripture class. He was also present on at least four, and often more, weekday evenings acting as a conductor of religious meetings and of the evening classes in reading, writing and accompts. He held many individual talks with scholars concerning their spiritual welfare and was kind and encouraging. He became a successful business man; David Stott consulted him on all school matters and they worked together in the greatest amity.

Braidley was completely different from David Stott. Physically imposing he was described as 'large and opulent with a ruffled shirt and a top-knot'; he was an orator, a 'Church and King' man, a singularly able accountant who 'wrote with a quill pen a hand which any of us might now envy, a writer in religious magazines and something of a poet'. He was considered a man of intellect, of gentlemanly bearing and Christian integrity. He was cheerful, affable and 'his always pleasing countenance' bore an 'ever-to-be-remembered smile'. He had limited schooling but a great deal of self-education thereafter, particularly in mathematics. He was well read and had learned several languages and played the flute. He never married.

Born in 1792 of respectable farming stock in the County of Durham, Braidley started his working life in a Manchester warehouse. At the age of 25 he went into partnership in a firm in New Cannon Street and he lived in Lever Street. He rapidly rose to wealth and the highest respect and influence. He took an interest in civic affairs, achieving the status of Boroughreeve of Manchester in 1831 and again in 1832, the only man who served two terms in the office. He also served as High Constable for the Hundred of Salford. 'At this time no man could stand higher in the estimation of his fellow-townsmen so much so that he was persuaded to stand for parliament, unsuccessfully contesting the seat of Manchester on behalf of the Conservatives on two occasions.

Braidley had a great concern for the health and morals of the working people and reported for the local physician and social investigator, James Philip Kay, on 'the number of persons entering a gin shop in five minutes, during eight successive Saturday evenings and at various periods from seven o'clock until ten'. Another of his concerns was the legislation to improve the condition of young people in factories. He was called to London several times to give evidence to parliament to influence the passing of bills.

In the midst of his public duties although unable to devote the amount of time to Bennett Street that he previously had, he did not forget the school and was always present on Sunday and whenever possible on Tuesday for the evening Bible class. In connection with his business interests he sailed to America in 1837, returning in November 1838. He had been away just twelve months and his letters record how he missed the school and its people. His absence from the teachers' Christmas party had 'cast an unusual gloom' and on his return the upper room of boys indulged in a 'simultaneous out-burst of joy' and clapping of hands.

His sojourn in America was followed by a lengthy stay in Wales. He lived there for several years, again for business reasons and wrote in 1840 of missing his old haunts and companions. On his return in 1844 his Bennett Street friends found him much changed in appearance and obviously ill. On the last evening of his life he attended St Paul's church and was found dead in his bed the following morning 3 April 1845. He was 52. In spite of the fact that he had been so active in the affairs of Manchester, his funeral took place in his home town of Sedgefield, County Durham.

4

1850-1870

The Heyday of the School

The period from 1850 until the 1870 Education Act was the heyday of Bennett Street Sunday School. It had become a large and complex organisation operating through the committee system set up in the 1820s and had progressed from providing simply religious instruction and elementary schooling to the establishment of a mechanics institute level of adult education.

Nationally the second half of the nineteenth century was a period of reform, social legislation and scientific invention. The Sunday School Movement was seen as unique throughout the country, its leaders being canvassed for their support of petitions to the House of Commons on subjects such as that for the 'better registration of public houses and other places of entertainment'. Parliamentary Acts included Education Acts, Factory Acts and the Parks for the People Act.

Manchester, much impressed by the Great Exhibition in London in 1851 mounted its own Art Treasures Exhibition in Old Trafford in 1857, the biggest temporary art exhibition ever held in Britain. Manchester's cultural scene also saw the founding in 1858 of the Hallé Orchestra, the world's first professional permanent orchestra, and in the same year a new market hall was erected in Swan Street near the school. In the 1860s the civic and commercial centre materialised with the laying out of Corporation Street, Portland Street and Albert Square. Contrasting with these symbols of Manchester's increasing economic importance, this was also the period during which disaster struck Lancashire, and the city, in the form of the Cotton Famine.[1]

For Bennett Street the 1850s had opened with two notable events. Firstly, Queen Victoria and the Prince Consort visited Manchester and Salford in 1851 and were treated to what the Queen, in her diary, referred to as the 'totally unprecedented sight' of 82,000 children drawn up in Peel Park to greet her. St Paul's Schools' Committee considered it a privilege to send 4,000 scholars from their various schools to join this throng and saw the additional expense involved as 'trifling'. Three thousand cups and medals in commemoration of this visit were distributed within Bennett Street[2]. Secondly, that same year, Bennett Street celebrated its own golden jubilee with a distribution of cups and medals.

The Building

The jubilee of the building itself was celebrated in 1868 with commemorative medals, a special service in church and a large reunion of former scholars. In the early 1850s at a time when there could be 400-500 young boys in No 2 room, that room was fitted with 'perforated glass for ventilation' and a decade later there is mention of a new classroom, with the intriguing footnote that the committee arranged for the 'substitution of a staircase in place of the present mode of entrance into [the] classroom'.[3]

The school's first almanack was published in 1861. An almanack is normally a type of annual hand-book, but Bennett Street's was printed on one large sheet of paper approximately two feet square and consisted of a calendar of church and school dates, details of officers, classes, societies, funds etc., and a list of benefactors. In 1863 2,500 copies were ordered and it was produced annually for the remainder of the school's life.

The Cotton Famine

Described by *The Times* as 'the Lancashire calamity', the Cotton Famine of 1861-65 was caused by the American Civil War and the consequent blockade on their ports; no American raw cotton could be shipped to this country and the Lancashire cotton industry ground to a complete halt. Cotton operatives were without work and wages. This in turn affected those with businesses dependent on them, such as corner shops. Other parts of the country remained unaffected and sent charitable donations in cash and kind for distribution by the Relief Committees set up in each affected town. Even decent hard-working families could become destitute; their possessions, furniture and clothing were successively sold or pawned until there was 'nothing for it but to take the relief'. Bennett Street's reaction to this unprecedented situation was firstly to take responsibility for a portion of St George's Parish (in which the school stood) in addition to that of St Paul's, and they also made a section of their building available to the local Relief Committee for its weekly distribution of food and clothing. The school also organised sewing classes to help occupy out-of-work females and this initiative in its turn provided much needed clothing and household items. Additional services were held on Sunday evenings for those 'who from want of clothing' felt unable to attend in the morning or afternoon. Sunday school rules of course demanded cleanliness and neatness from those attending and during the Cotton Famine they had no 'Sunday best' clothes. Fund raising concerts were given and there was a collection in school once a month for the Relief Committee.

Anniversary Sunday

By the 1850s Anniversary Sunday had become a red-letter day. A special evening service was held in church with a visiting preacher and the choir augmented by old school members. After a short service at the Sunday afternoon gathering in school, the all-important collection was made by direct giving – 'sending the cap round'. This money, although given in by scholars and teachers, was raised by them from local shops and businesses, relatives, neighbours and friends who might (or who might not) have an interest in the school but who were willing to donate small amounts to please the collector. At a later date collecting cards were issued in advance of the day and the names of the donors and the amounts given were recorded. The school acknowledged that such gifts were usually small but such small-scale giving amassed about £136 in 1850; this augmented the sum received via the subscription list which that year amounted to around £149. One memory of anniversary Sunday in the 1850s is recorded:

'[Anniversary Sunday] was the day in which all the love for the old School broke out in the wildest enthusiasm, from the men whose heads had whitened in the service of the Lord in these Schools, down to the impulsive little lad who had spent a good part of his Saturday holiday in converting the pennies he had begged for the School into farthings, that he might have the more frequent gratifications of giving. It was a delightful day to us young lads, for there was a relaxed discipline in the School on that afternoon...the scholars were allowed to go about in small guerrilla parties to attack any old scholars they happened to know, or any more pliable material who might happen to be keeping company with one of their sisters to augment the amount collected in their own particular class...

...Tea over and the totals of the collection [known], now we were all anxious to secure a seat in Church. What a grand sight was the choir ...[it] always overflowed its banks on these occasions and the ordinary seat holders...were obliged to make room...[for] old choristers' [as they prepared for] the opening notes of that noble paraphrase of the twenty-fourth Psalm, "Lift up your heads"...'.[4]

Religion

The leaders declared that 'religion and the common affairs of life run side by side, as they should do'. Sunday lessons in the 1850s/60s included subjects such as gospel history and the Hebrew monarchy. Examinations were taken. An adult Bible class was set up in 1861 and at the other end of the age range, there is the first mention of a Sunday infant school; the Tract Society continued to flourish. In 1860 twenty-four teachers signed a formal request for permission to establish a branch of the Band of Hope.[5] The Bennett Street branch became an enduring enterprise, flourishing alone for twenty years before having a branch of the Church of England Temperance Society joined with it.

The male teachers started to meet on Sunday mornings from 8am until 9am before their Sunday school duties, for scripture reading and instruction; the females had similar classes on a Tuesday evening. The numbers attending the Sunday school afternoon service were always greater than those in the morning, by as many as 300 scholars in the 1850s. It was quite customary at Bennett Street for females to be more numerous than males, a situation considered somewhat unusual in the Sunday School Movement as a whole; normally it was boys who were sent to Sunday school to take advantage of the free reading and writing classes. At Bennett Street boys were said to be more 'in/out', but girls were more 'lasting'.

Having been singing from 'Hymns for the use of the Sunday Schools in Manchester' since 1839, in 1868 Bennett Street sought to supplement this hymnal by publishing their own which was always referred to as 'the small hymn book'; it measured only 2¾ x 4¼ inches and ran to at least six editions, the sixth being printed in 1896. Included in it are the words of 'the Canticle' which perhaps more than any other became Bennett Street's own school song; it is first mentioned as being sung at the Christmas Day Party in 1862; 'A Happy, Happy Christmas and a Merry Bright New Year', and was sung at festive season services and parties thereafter. In addition to hymns the small hymn book contained a simplified service based on the Book of Common Prayer and included a prayer, 'Bless all poor, outcast children and those who have none to teach them'.[6]

Education

In an address in 1851 the rector stated that universal opinion was 'now' in favour of education, and an essay from the Literary and Educational Society's Odds and Ends magazine of 1866 listed various advantages of compulsory education, its author concluding that 'I have not been able to find any very serious disadvantages'.

At this period the school was described as being surrounded by factories with a large population crowding the neighbouring streets and alleys. The leaders were of the opinion that the Sunday learning and the evening classes they offered were both indispensable as during the week a large proportion of this population was employed in these factories. And so in 1862 they made the school's educational facilities available to non-members also, provided they were recommended by a school member.

The evening curriculum was extended to include algebra, elocution and essay writing. A tonic sol-fa class, (a popular method of music learning at the time) and a boys' music class also operated in the 1860s, but the request to form a drum and fife band was vetoed. Weekly classes in plain sewing and housewifery for teachers and older scholars proved a popular innovation. Special evening classes in scripture and general subjects targeted at teachers and senior scholars had started in 1850 so that, together with the reading room, the library and the benefit societies, the school considered they were providing 'every advantage of a mechanics institute but one that operated on Christian principles'.

Around ten per cent (240) of the scholar membership attended Bennett Street's Writing School in the 1850s, a figure which steadily decreased until, in 1857, the figure dropped to below 100 for the first time. Of the 166 teachers on the roll in 1855, twenty-nine were registered as learners in the writing classes, a figure which by the end of the decade had reduced to eight. No further statistics regarding teachers as learner-writers appear after this date. Also attending the reading and writing classes were 'men of middle age, many of whom from various causes [have] forgotten the learning they once acquired'. During this period instructions were issued for the revision of the spelling book, indicating that the school perhaps had published its own.

During the 1850s thirty per cent of the membership were subscribing to the Library. This became a free library during the 1860s, as further municipal free libraries were opening in the vicinity[7].

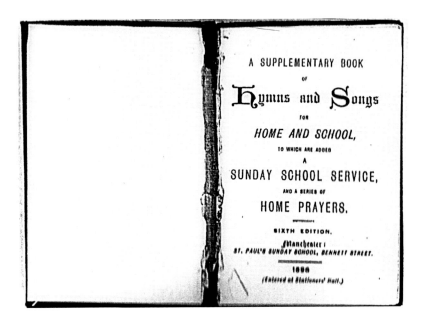

A SUPPLEMENTARY BOOK

OF

Hymns and Songs

FOR

HOME AND SCHOOL,

TO WHICH ARE ADDED

A

SUNDAY SCHOOL SERVICE,

AND A SERIES OF

HOME PRAYERS.

SIXTH EDITION.

Manchester:
ST. PAUL'S SUNDAY SCHOOL, BENNETT STREET.

1896

(Entered at Stationers' Hall.)

---

114   Ancient Carol.

A HAPPY, happy Christmas, and a merry
   bright New Year,
How sweet the kind old greetings sound to
   every heart and ear ;
No matter how care-burthen'd, and no
   matter how deprest,
A something in their welcome makes them
   dear to every breast.

We heard them in our childhood, when with
   spirits light and gay,
We dreamt not that life's joyfulness could
   ever pass away ;
And though long years of carefulness have
   sober'd many a heart ;
A joy still lingers round them which can
   never quite depart.

Nor ever shall—if, Christian-like, we count
   the rolling years,
Not as removing joys from us, but sins, and
   cares, and tears :
And upward, onward, bearing us to that
   bright land and blest,
Where the wicked cease from troubling, and
   the weary are at rest.

No year can open gloomily for him whose
   heart doth yearn,
Above all hopes and cares on earth, to see
   his Lord's return ;
As stars their light, and mists their shade,
   lay down before the day,
So joys and griefs of earth in Heav'n's calm
   sunshine fade away.

Good friends ! would you with happiness
   the op'ning year begin ?
Come kneel by Jesu's cradle-bed, and count
   the cost of sin ;
Then let the year its colouring of sober duty
   take ;
Rise up, go forth—do everything, for your
   dear Saviour's sake.

No matter how care-burthen'd, and no
   matter how deprest,
A something in their welcome makes them
   dear to every breast.
Long may the kind old greetings sound to
   every heart and ear,
A happy, happy Christmas, and a merry
   bright New Year.

Adapted from F. S. B. Monsell, LL.D.

A Canticle for Christmas

Penny Readings, (poetry or prose usually of an uplifting or cultural nature and intended as an alternative type of entertainment to that available in public houses) were also started in the school at this time. They were cheap to attend.

The Lit

The Literary and Educational Society had become Bennett Street's foremost adult society providing both educational stimulus and social interaction for the young men. George Milner, who rose through the school from scholar to Trustee, was its mainstay for over fifty years. A twentieth century president voiced his opinion that it was Milner who had made the society a centre of culture in the Manchester of the late nineteenth century. It met weekly on Friday evenings and the records show that other lettings for Friday evening were accepted only provided they 'did not interfere with the Lit'.[8]

The Odds And Ends Magazine

The Literary Society's syllabus was enhanced by the production each year of their 'Odds and Ends' manuscript magazine. Compiled annually from 1855 to 1962, the contents were the original work of the members themselves who were described as 'being drawn from all sections of town workers: workers at the loom and desk; in the mill, the shop and the warehouse'. There was the very occasional guest contributor such as Charles Rowley the Ancoats philanthropist and much later L S Lowry the artist. The articles, handwritten by their authors onto the specially prepared hand-made paper, covered contemporary events of national importance such as the Crimean war or the abolition of the slave trade. Discussions of fine arts were included as were literary criticism, tours (that is holidays), biographical sketches, original poetry and 'pieces of a lighter character'. The contributions, which could extend to 300 pages or more, were bound into one volume each year. These volumes were described as 'profusely, and in some instances elaborately, illustrated with pen and ink sketches, drawings and photographs'. One evening of each session was devoted to the ceremony of presenting the new volume to the society.[9]

Prizes

Contrary to what might be expected, Bennett Street's first benefactor was not from the more affluent class but from its own membership. William Tuke died aged twenty-five in 1861; the records do not say he was a teacher; he is simply described as a member of the school. Orphaned at the age of fourteen he became a foreman in the plumbing trade and left the sum of £10, later described as 'a large part of his scanty and hard won savings' to his 'much loved School'. This was used for a boys' prize for proficiency in scriptural knowledge and was still being awarded after World War II. William Tuke paved the way for the steady stream of legacies and endowments of later years.[10]

Welfare and Charity

The necessity of maintaining a respectable image on a small income was a constant source of concern. In 1851 David Stott's original welfare provision for children was extended to include an Adult Sick and Funeral Society. This was considered desirable as it helped remove 'the necessity for the young men joining societies held in public houses.' The children's society, established in 1812, and by this time better known as the half-penny club, was still being conducted with 'vigour and success', with around 50% of the children subscribing to it. Weekly subscriptions to the Funeral Society were raised from a farthing to a ha'penny and to the Sick Society from a ha'penny to one penny. Payments of between half-a-crown and five shillings were paid out for each week of a member's inability to work.

A penny savings bank was started in 1851; it opened on a Monday evening on school premises and was open 'to the neighbourhood at large...irrespective of their religious professions'. In 1862 permission was granted for a building society to be opened in the school. The remarkable success of the school's financial societies was considered to be the result of having to deal with a 'frugal and temperate' class. They claimed around 300 members in 1855 and in 1880 over 1,000, the latter figure including scholars, teachers, leaders, wives and widows.[11]

Charitable collections during the period, in addition to those for the customary causes such as the British and Foreign Bible Society, included that towards a statue of Queen Victoria to be erected in Salford and, on home ground in 1852, fund raising included the sale in school of prints of an engraving of David Stott at one or two shillings each; the membership also presented a concert to benefit the widow and children of a recently deceased teacher.

Whit Week

On Whit Monday it had become the custom for the children to wear white, in order to distinguish them from the non-religious processions of the early nineteenth century when 'drab' colours were worn.

Immediately after the end of the Cotton Famine, in 1866, the duration of the Whit Week outings was curtailed, the timings changing from 8am until 7pm rather than from 7am until 8pm. A plain breakfast was provided for the teachers on the day of the scholars' outing, and the venues were more local (the children required just 'a field to play in') and the school started to use the new Manchester parks for some of their adult excursions; in 1866 the teachers were conveyed by horse-drawn omnibuses to the Botanic Gardens in West Manchester and the scholars were taken to view the Workman's Art Exhibition at the Royal Institution (1,000 tickets at a penny each).

But railway outings remained the favourite excursion although cost at this juncture was a priority. In 1854 following protracted but unsuccessful negotiations over ticket prices (the railway wished to charge scholars over fourteen years of age at the same rate as the teachers) a rail outing was changed at the eleventh hour to a boat trip on the Bridgewater Canal to Worsley or Dunham. In 1863 a teachers' outing to Prestbury was arranged 'if the fare does not exceed one shilling, or should the price be more than one shilling, to Lymm for ten pence'. In Whit Week 1867, shortly after the end of the famine the committee was casting around for 'anywhere to go for tenpence?'

This was a period when various railway companies wooed institutions that might organise group excursions. For several years the Manchester Sheffield and Lincolnshire Railway Company held an 'Excursion for Trip Promoters'; in 1860 they allocated to St Paul's church nineteen first-class tickets and thirty-nine covered carriage tickets for distribution in the Turner Street and Bennett Street Schools; these tickets were allocated to the clergy, the Visitors and the superintendents and on occasion extended to some teachers of the boys' rooms, but not apparently to those of the girls'. Unusually, the Committee of Management organised an excursion of their own to 'Handforth for Styal' in July 1868.

Social Activities

By the 1850s the Christmas Day Tea had become a more formal 'treat' for the teachers in recognition of their year's service in the school, with printed invitations being issued to the 'teachers and their wives':

'The Visitors of Bennett Street request the pleasure of the Company of ….to Tea in the School on Christmas Day at half past 5 o'clock'.

This wording assumes that all teachers were male; this was not the case but the evidence is that female teachers did seem to retire from office when they married. Priced tickets for other invited friends, or 'strangers' as they were called, were available; these tickets were priced at one shilling in 1852. The event followed a regular pattern of an evening of individual musical items with carols sung by everybody. At this point, after fifty years of the school's existence leaders were becoming eligible for long service awards which were often presented on these occasions.

The other parties of the festive season continued to be over-subscribed, 'want of room' preventing admission of all those who wished to attend (1854), 400 tickets being considered the maximum for safety. Perhaps this was one of the reasons why in 1864 a 'juvenile party' is mentioned for the first time. All parties aimed to be self-supporting and, contrary to their normal rules, immediately after the end of the famine the Committee of Management gave free tickets to some of the teachers for the New Year parties.

During the period of the Cotton Famine, Bennett Street's scholar numbers had decreased by almost 1,000. As the 1860s drew to a close and with the Education Bill going through parliament, the Bennett Street leaders were well aware that the needs of their members would change.

5

1870-1900

After the Education Act

The passing of the Education Act in 1870, the government's first move towards compulsory (although not free) primary education, inevitably proved to be a watershed in the activities of Bennett Street Sunday School.

The period also included Queen Victoria's Golden Jubilee in 1887 and her Diamond Jubilee in 1897. It was an era of exploration, for instance to Africa, and of invention, for example of x-rays in 1896. At home the Bank Holiday Act (1871) gave six Bank Holidays a year. The centenary of the Sunday School Movement was commemorated in 1880.

The centre of Manchester changed in a fundamental way; the Town Hall was built during the 1870s, municipal libraries and reading rooms were established and the Ship Canal was opened in 1894. Much of the poor housing surrounding the school was cleared in 1892 and although some was replaced by the Victoria Square tenements, the area had largely become 'a parish of railways, mills, warehouses and a great market'. Less residential property meant fewer children to attend Bennett Street.

St Paul's church on Turner Street was demolished; when built in 1765 it had been situated among fields and gardens but by the 1870s was surrounded by large warehouses. A new church, built largely from the materials of the old, was consecrated in 1878 on Oldham Road near the Swan Street junction, much closer to the school. A subsequent re-arrangement of neighbouring parishes brought Bennett Street Sunday School finally into the parish of St Paul's.[1]

Anticipating the withdrawal of secular education from Sunday schools, Bennett Street's leaders had formulated a new policy. They proposed to concentrate on religious instruction whilst continuing to encourage social activities. Innovations included the establishment of adult Sunday classes, the formation of the 'select class' from which teachers would be drawn (1871), and the inauguration of Founder's Day (1894). The Literary Society expanded to include female members.

Centenary of the Sunday School Movement

The centenary of the Sunday School Movement (1880) was celebrated nationally, the school's commemorative project being the publication of a history of the school, together with eulogies of the founder and early workers. Bennett Street celebrations always included a special church service, but on this occasion the rector organised a series of services with sermons preached by seven clergymen who had been Bennett Street scholars[2]. The customary parties were organised and medals bearing portraits of Robert Raikes and of the school were commissioned, as was a gill pot displaying the heads of Raikes and David Stott. In addition they took advantage of photography becoming more commercially available and organised a group portrait of the leaders.

———— * ————

Uncharacteristically, Queen Victoria's Golden Jubilee in 1887 was not celebrated by Bennett Street as the committee found it 'impracticable to provide a demonstration' but on the following Whit Monday jubilee medals were worn by the 2,000 members walking in the procession.

The inauguration of Founder's Day occurred in 1894, the aim being to keep the memory of David Stott alive and to provide an occasion for a re-union of former members. It took place each September on a date near to David Stott's birthday. The central feature was the delivery of a eulogy of David Stott and of other Bennett Street worthies. Founder's Day also became one of the occasions when long service was recognised by the presentation of diocesan medals and by the presentation of portraits and testimonials to those achieving fifty years of service. A programme of musical items was always included, the proceedings opening and closing with a hymn and the assembly being dismissed with the Benediction. Founder's Day was last held in 1939.[3]

The Quiver Medals

A momentous occasion in the annals of Bennett Street took place during this period - the presentation of Quiver medals. *The Quiver* was a London-based monthly magazine with a philanthropic bias, self-styled 'for Sunday and General Reading'. To commemorate Queen Victoria's Diamond Jubilee in 1897, it launched a county-by-county project drawing attention to the voluntary work of Sunday school teachers of every denomination. Awards were made to those who had given at least twenty years of continuous service and were still active in the same institution. The magazine recorded that:

'The Special Silver Medal and Presentation Bible for the longest service in Lancashire..... has been gained by

Mr Samuel Goodwin…who has a record of 58 years' continuous service at St Paul's Sunday School Bennett Street Manchester'.

A further forty-four Bennett Street superintendents and teachers (five of them women) received bronze medals for service of between twenty and fifty-two years. Quiver medals showed a seated female figure clad in Grecian draperies with children seated round her feet. Such external recognition was almost unheard of and offered a further opportunity for a ceremony of congratulatory and nostalgic speeches. The presentations were made in school on March 1st 1898 by the Dean of Manchester and a photographic montage of those honoured was subsequently hung in the School.[4]

The Building

In 1889 the leaders voiced their regrets that inadequacies in the building prevented them from offering scientific education. They felt the need for more classrooms, a large lecture room and a gymnasium, and commissioned architects to draw up the necessary plans. To achieve such expansion they attempted to acquire adjacent land fronting onto Oldham Road and also enquired about purchasing the Sunday school site. The funding of such an enterprise was not considered insuperable as they had the greatest confidence that their members and the school's many friends throughout the country would provide the necessary finance – as had always happened in the past. Neither of these projects came to fruition at this point although a new wing was built within the existing school land early in the twentieth century. The purchase of the school site never materialised.

The acquisition of new equipment and furniture was a rare event but in 1898 a handsome reading desk (a pulpit) of carved oak was presented to No 2 room in memory of William Rostron, a former manager, by his son.

Rules

The strict enforcement of school rules on discipline and behaviour seems to have been effective; records of bad conduct brought to the notice of the committee are sparse. The shaming method during the 1870s, when there were 1,557 scholars on the roll, was that bad conduct was 'called from the desk' in each room and culprits subsequently brought before the committee. Two scholars were expelled for unexplained misconduct on a Whit Friday trip; shouting and *ad hoc* games of football outside the entrance on a Sunday were condemned and a new rule confined smoking in school to the passages (1893) and in 1898 it was prohibited in the school as a whole. The committee did not agree with the use of 'corporal punishment of any kind whatsoever', and teachers (particularly those in the older boys' room) were instructed to refrain from its use. Dancing was not permitted; when the Lit applied for permission to include the word 'dancing' in one of their announcements, the committee considered the matter 'fully' but rejected the application; nor was dancing permitted at outside lets which were now considered – there being less pressure on space after 1870.

Anniversary Sunday

The anniversary collection usually resulted in a figure of around £300 at this period; in 1875 it raised £324 1s 8d. Anniversary was the occasion when the subscribers were contacted, but even at the latter end of the nineteenth century their subscriptions amounted only to about ten per cent of the final total. Few large subscriptions were received after 1880.

Fund Raising

In 1884 the school took the decision to invest in dwelling houses rather than in the building societies, and so rents joined donations, legacies and room lettings as a source of income. One outside let during this period was for meetings concerned with the promotion of a ship canal. During the 1890s the school followed the fashion of holding fund-raising bazaars, firstly for the church organ fund, and in 1891 for the school benevolent fund. The latter, opened by the Recorder of Salford was not well patronised by the public but £764 15s 2½d was raised from 'church and school pockets'. Decorating the room like a Chinese market (again following a current trend) was only a limited success as 'our good old School does not lend itself very well to spectacular display'.

Religion

One of the earliest reactions to the Education Act had been a short-lived experiment to start a ragged school on a Sunday evening. It was not a success and operated for only three months in 1871. The more lasting reaction was the decision to concentrate on religious education. It had become apparent that the Sunday scholars were 'not as eager now they are educated and working' and so a certain amount of reorganisation took place. The New Testament was used for the morning classes, the Old Testament in the afternoons and all classes worked towards ruri-decanal examinations using the diocesan scheme of lessons. A more participative system was started whereby the older boys delivered the lesson themselves and followed it with discussion. In an attempt to provide brighter Sundays, services of song were organised and also short lectures on sacred composers illustrated by musical selections. The leaders always wished scholars to benefit not only from religion and education but also from 'culture brought to their notice'.

The new rector voiced his concern regarding lapses in church attendance. The policy at this stage was that classes attended church by rotation, odd numbered classes alternating weekly with evens. Investigation revealed that the older boys objected to mixed-sex processing to church and so the arrangements were changed, male classes alternating with female classes. The rector also arranged an afternoon service on every fifth Sunday of the month to enable all the school to attend church together. Quarterly devotional meetings prior to communion were instituted and a communicants' union was established in 1898; sixty-four candidates were subsequently presented for confirmation, the local press reporting that this was the highest number from any Manchester parish.[5]

From the 1870s, with the day school being inspected by the Manchester Education authorities, the Committee of Management requested that the Sunday school be inspected by the Cathedral authorities. Following his inspection in 1876, the Dean of Manchester noted 'the abundance of Teachers is a striking feature'. But the new daytime education had changed the role of the Sunday school teacher. It had long been the boast at Bennett Street that teacher supply always exceeded demand; the early experience of lack of assistance from the influential classes had been perpetuated and it remained the case that the vast majority of teachers were appointed from within the school. By 1880 almost all the officers too had been scholars; not only had scholars become teachers and superintendents but some had achieved the status of Visitors and trustees. But (and it was a large but) many of them had not received an external education; educationally their scholars were catching up with them, and indeed overtaking them. The leaders recognised that teachers' loyalty alone was insufficient in the new climate.

Originally teachers had taught elementary reading and writing and had held a pastoral role, visiting their scholars in times of trouble and also playing a part in helping them to obtain employment. As early as 1853, in order to prevent the appointment of 'unfit persons', the committee had started a class to prepare prospective teachers for their role. In the altered circumstances of the 1870s a special Sunday 'select class' was formed to accommodate such teachers-in-waiting who then served a twelve month probationary period before being formally appointed. In 1888 there were 119 males and 56 females in the class and discussions took place on 'what to teach and how'. For the following thirty years teachers' scripture classes were held, diocesan examinations taken voluntarily and prizes awarded. In 1893 the Lit was charged with conducting a systematic teachers' training course. In the 1890s recruitment of teachers became more difficult, partly because of the increased knowledge and training required but also because by 1889 it was noted that a large number of teachers and scholars were travelling distances of several miles to attend with 'not a few having to make a railway journey'.

Not all adults were teachers or members of the select class; many remained as scholars. 'The difficulty of retaining elder scholars, so much spoken of elsewhere is not felt at all at Bennett Street'. The school 'tried above all other things to keep together their young men', believing that joining in school activities and mixing with those who had 'already made their way' was far better for their welfare than cultivating 'less advantageous' friendships elsewhere.[6]

In 1880 out of 1,445 scholars, 300 were adults (120 men and 180 women) a far higher proportion than was the norm for most Sunday schools and it was the rector who suggested that an adult male class be formed. There had been a similar class in 1861 which had met on a Sunday morning but numbers had never been large. This new group however, for men over twenty-one and especially for parents, met on Sunday afternoons, had its own separate room and was much more successful.

By 1874 a larger room was required and by 1880 there were about 120 members. They met for Bible reading and discussion led by senior teachers; they had their own book and rambling clubs, their own social events and they organised the visiting of their sick or absent members by a 'committee of [our] own body' rather than by teachers or leaders, the method necessarily adopted for the younger scholars. Another sign of their being of an older age group was that they requested hymn books with larger type! It was considered a 'most successful Working Men's Club' and became a great strength within the school.[7]

Firm friendships were forged at Bennett Street, some of the young men banding themselves together into a 'clan'. There were at least three of these clans over the years; the first mentioned is in 1883 when it booked one of the school's rooms for a private party and there were a further two active during the interwar years, one of which features in the dedication of this history.

Records of the 1870s reveal that in addition to former teachers and scholars visiting on Sunday afternoons, those in authority at other schools, from other cities and even from other countries called in at this 'excellent Sabbath school'. In 1870 an atmosphere of 'peculiar vitality' in the school was recorded, and the Bishop, addressing the adult room tea party, spoke of the talent and the moral good being cultivated in what he termed 'a somewhat benighted district'. The editor of *The Manchester Guardian,* C P Scott MP, speaking at the men's class social party saw Bennett Street as a centre of self-culture, self-help and mutual assistance and exhorted the members to:-

'go on with courage and with charity and prosper, and confer increasing benefits upon this district, which God knows, needs all the benefits you can confer upon it'.[8]

Education

In 1889 the *Manchester Guardian* reported that schemes for [nation-wide] evening schools were under discussion and commented that 'long before the idea of continuation classes had entered the public mind Bennett Street was hard at work with them'. New admissions to the evening classes as early as 1872 were recorded as 194 boys and 197 girls, and during the next decade the evening classes for reading, writing and arithmetic were well attended, 281 readers and writers being recorded in 1875. With the increase in municipal provision, all classes were condensed into three evenings per week with music, drawing, ornamental writing, phono-graphy, languages and 'mathematics etc.' being transferred to the Manchester Education Department in 1881. English, bookkeeping and shorthand were taught by school leaders and these classes were retained. The writing school operated until at least 1881, the numbers falling steadily at a rate to be expected in the changing circumstances. So with the Lit occupying its accustomed slot on Fridays, the weekday evenings remained a hive of activity, the committee confessing that 'the gas is scarcely ever turned out before 10pm'.[9]

The only record of the teaching which survives in the archives is that of George Milner's English classes. His notebook records that in 1885 he was teaching from *The History of English Language and Literature,* published by Chambers at one shilling and sixpence and that the grammar lessons included parsing and composition, defining the parts of speech and discussing the formation of clauses and sentences. The class was studying Shakespeare's *Much Ado about Nothing* and *In Memoriam and other poems* by Tennyson, the Poet Laureate. An annual internal examination was taken at Easter. Two questions from the 1886 paper were:

'Qu. 8. What are the general characteristics of Tennyson's Poetry?

Qu.13. What proof is there in this play [*Much Ado about Nothing*] that Shakespeare appealed to a popular audience and to an educated one?'[10]

At this period higher education for the working class was virtually unknown but Bennett Street fostered any ambitions. A scholar who left to go away to college in 1879 was presented with a suitable collection of books, and in 1897 John Grantham, a Manchester alderman and a Bennett Street Visitor, invested £1,000 to found six scholarships of three years each at Manchester School of Technology, which they said, 'ran several courses of university standard'. These scholarships were for any of the 'Tech's' evening classes; the money, £5 per annum, was to cover fees and books with any remaining balance being handed over to the student in cash. They were open to male scholars between the ages of thirteen and twenty-one who had been attending Bennett Street for at least three years. Twenty-nine young men competed for the first six scholarships.

The Lit

The Lit had become Bennett Street's foremost adult society providing both educational stimulus and social interaction between young men and women; in 1875 there were 201 members of whom forty-five were women. The Lit was found to be successful in retaining the interest of those (of both sexes) who might otherwise desert the Sunday school culture during their adolescence and early adulthood. It was noted too in the 1880s that contributing to the *Odds and Ends* Magazine helped members to write English 'with no inconsiderable ability'. Although originally intended only to appear in manuscript, two volumes of selections were subsequently printed and published.

Rather than follow the current school fashion for tea parties, the Lit maintained its reputation for 'recreation of a higher kind' by organising a series of conversazioni, the chief features of which included music, the display of pictures, dramatic recitals and conversation. A Manchester journalist, John H Nodal, who was not connected with Bennett Street, described the Lit's syllabus in 1880 as a masterpiece of far-sighted organisation, voicing his opinion that it indicated 'an industry in the pursuit of knowledge of which we know no parallel'. Others voiced doubts as to whether the intellectual training available could match such an extensive programme.[11]

In spite of municipal branch libraries and reading rooms having opened as near as Ancoats and Rochdale Road during this period, Bennett Street continued to add new books to its own library and reacted to the controversial subject of Sunday opening by extending its hours. In addition to twice weekly opening on Monday and Thursday evenings, the leaders arranged for 200 library books to be available in each room on a Sunday afternoon. When, in 1885, New Testaments were bought for school use, a supply was also allocated for sale at one penny each.

Prizes

From the 1870s onwards special prizes endowed by members or by legacies were awarded, for example to the select class for attendance and conduct; to the upper room of boys for the 'tasteful rendering of sacred music'. In addition to the teachers' annual prize, those achieving twenty years' service were each presented with a Bible. At a presentation in 1893 the prizes were described as being of the 'best literature' 'prettily bound', and memories were evoked of earlier years when 'covers of blue sugar paper' had enclosed contents as 'unattractive as their exteriors'.[12]

Although always supportive of literature, the leaders seem to have had a somewhat ambivalent attitude to music; various early attempts to hold singing classes were short-lived. Although there is no evidence of a school choir, the Band of Hope ran a choral society and there is brief reference to an orchestral society in the 1880s.

In 1893 the committee did agree to the formation of a singing class but would accept no financial responsibility for it. This may have been the first move towards the formal founding of the Orpheus Glee Club in 1897 which, although not strictly a school organisation did rehearse on school premises and was conducted by a Bennett Street man. It became well-known and by 1904 had 'engaged in thirty-five competitions with leading musical societies in other parts of the kingdom, and it has taken first honours on twenty-one of these occasions'. The Orpheus was in great demand to give concerts at Bennett Street and elsewhere and was in existence until the Second World War.[13]

Welfare

Poverty was still rife and the school's social welfare network continued to fulfil a need; 'the closest Victorians came to having ...social services was...[through] voluntary organizations mainly inspired by religious motives'. When one Bennett Street family found itself entirely without food they discovered 'a large loaf and a small amount of money' left anonymously on their window sill. The school's Sick and Funeral Society continued to grow and when its Benevolent Fund was formed in 1881, the inclusion of non-school members was specifically mentioned, its aim being to deal 'privately with ...cases of distress and hardship [as distinct from sickness and death] arising amongst our parishioners and school folk'. In one year aid in kind (food, medicine and clothing) was given to twenty-six members of the

Band of Hope; Christmas parcels were sent to less prosperous members; a free breakfast on Christmas morning was provided for poor scholars; and the children's holiday fund sent seventeen to Tabley for a three week stay in the Cheshire countryside. But not all were in penury, in 1880 there were 1,500 depositors using the Penny Bank and in addition to their normal charitable collections, the Christmas party of 1900 collected money to support troops fighting in the Boer War.[14]

An extension to the welfare network was the free Employment Registry started in 1886. This was a type of private 'situations wanted' column. It was printed in the school's magazine and aimed to match up a list of unemployed members with 'persons of influence in the schools' who required workers, or who could make recommendations to others who did. It was seen as a formalisation of a duty previously carried out informally by the teachers and in its new form was also available to non-school members.

Whit Week

The outdoor venue for the Whit Monday procession was changed in 1878 from St Ann's Square to Albert Square which had been laid out during the 1860s; the Bennett Street contingent at this point was led by bands from either a temperance society or a railway company.

The Whit-week railway outings flourished. In 1872 the organisers, perceiving danger in the scholars' trip by railway wagon proposed that in future the accommodation should be upgraded but that the trip should be shorter so that it remained within the price range; chosen destinations included Clayton Bridge from where the children walked to fields in Droylsden; and on another occasion 300 travelled by rail to Lower Crumpsall. It must be said that a scholar's view of the wagon trip differed somewhat from that of the leaders:

'We think a great deal of the intensity of the delight of the trip is taken away by the substitution of ordinary railway carriages for the old cattle trucks. In the latter conveyances you were so close together, and if it happened to rain, it was only like watering a lot of cabbages. Besides, in the trucks you had no patent spring buffers, and it was such fun to be bumped about a bit, and if you lost a few teeth, they must have been loose ones…It was awfully jolly in the tunnels in a truck; it was so nice and dark, and you appeared to get a good many more bumps that you did in the open…you could hold your face up and count how many drops of wet fell on it as you passed through'.[15]

Around this time objections were raised in Manchester regarding the principle of Whit Week outings for scholars, but Bennett Street leaders defended them robustly:

'Those who oppose them frequently know nothing of the real condition of the poor, and of the hard, monotonous lives which their children necessarily lead. To such as these Whitsuntide is the brightest spot in the year'.[16]

During the 1870s the children's sports day also included the crowning of the May queen. Beginning in 1872, this event quickly became immensely popular and attracted vast crowds. In 1877 when it was staged in a field in Blackley there were said to be 'some ten thousand spectators'. This 'startle[d] the managers'; the situation had grown beyond their control and the event was regretfully discontinued.[17]

Although their outings were normally confined to Whit Week, in 1887 both the day and Sunday scholars were taken to view an exhibition of industrial products manufactured by firms in the Manchester area; this was staged at Old Trafford to mark Queen Victoria's golden jubilee, and was opened by the Prince of Wales. The children travelled by train and at the end of their journey were supplied with free buns, tea, coffee and cocoa.

During the 1870s/80s the adults undertook Whit Week train journeys for half-day outings to such destinations as Didsbury, Greenfield or to Cheadle Hulme prior to walking to Bramall Hall; their full day outings included the Wrekin, Southport, Lytham and Windermere. In response to Cambrian Rail's advertisements of 'beautiful places on the line', in 1890s they added Llangollen, Barmouth and Betws-y-Coed to their venues. It was during the visit to Betws-y-Coed in 1893 that near-tragedy struck the party. Two scholars fell into deep water and were rescued by William Ashton, a teacher in No 2 room and Andrew Dean of the select class who 'at once jumped after them and brought them safely to land'. For this action Ashton and Dean were awarded Certificates from the Royal Humane Society; these were presented to them in school by the Lord Mayor of Manchester. Implicit gratitude to the school's swimming club which had been started in 1888 can be assumed, and can it be coincidence that life saving classes started in 1893?

Social Activities

With the passing of the Bank Holiday Act in 1871 members' leisure time increased and the Bennett Street social scene expanded to fill the new recreational need. It was in fact possible to spend all one's spare time at school in 'wholesome employment'. Temperance remained an issue and in 1871 an external petition to close public houses on Sundays was available in school for signature. The Band of Hope continued their activities into the twentieth century, organising varied events such as concerts, Christy Minstrels and swimming galas, and in 1888 they held an exhibition of 'objects of interest and curiosity' which was the forerunner of a series of Industrial Exhibitions held under the auspices of the Committee of Management from 1889.

These Industrial Exhibitions, held during the 1880s and 1890s, fulfilled all the Bennett Street objectives; as well as being social occasions they were educational and cultural, and they raised funds. Perhaps best described as a village show held within a town, the declared purpose was to:

'create, foster, and encourage in the people of the School and neighbourhood a taste for the higher branches of their own trades or occupations'

The competitive classes included the following (two examples of each class are given but there were many more).

Handicrafts: woodwork, glass cutting/blowing (Ancoats was the home of a large glass industry);
arts and decorations: wallpaper designs, photography;
educational: penmanship, freehand drawing;
needlework: embroidery of flannel petticoats, the washing, starching and ironing of fronts, collars and cuffs;
cookery: homemade bread, jellies;
window gardening: 'best single hyacinth any colour, in bloom', best fern case.

The third exhibition, held over three days in 1890 distributed total prize money of £40; special entertainments were presented and a refreshment buffet provided. A sale of work was held each evening 'in aid of poor and necessitous scholars' as the Benevolent Committee estimated that £20 would be required to meet the demands that would be made upon it that year.[18]

This was the high era of the tea party. By 1870 the Christmas Day teachers' party had moved to 26 December. On one occasion when it was held on Christmas Eve excerpts from *Messiah* and Bible readings replaced the usual musical items. This party, the New Year parties and the parents' party were all organised centrally; in addition each evening class, each Sunday room, even each class within each room, all held an annual tea, as did the body of teachers. Even those who decorated the room for the Christmas season had a party of their own; no-one else attended and it was held when they took the Christmas decorations down. There is no evidence of a charge for room hire for internal parties although permission from the committee was required. This was readily given and included use of 'tea apparatus'. The organisers of the individual parties were also responsible for paying the caretaker for the washing of the table cloths and towels.

The New Year parties continued to be very popular; the words 'Tea on the table at 5.30' meant a sit-down meat tea with bread and butter, various savoury accompaniments and sweet bread and cake. To help the sub-committees catering for these large parties the Committee of Management prepared a scale of food quantities and in 1895 made what they considered a thoughtful labour-saving suggestion - the purchase of a bread cutting machine; but 'most of the No 4 teachers objected to it'. From 1867 humorous sketches were gradually added to the musical entertainment; the managers thought the length of the entertainment 'too long by one-third' in 1887!

The parents' party, the occasion when the relatives of both the day and Sunday scholars were invited into the school, was an annual event normally held on a weekday evening in October. To help achieve maximum attendance advertisements were placed in the local press (the *Manchester Guardian* and *Examiner*, the *City News* and the *Courier*). Following a tea, addresses were given on the present position of both schools and their prospects for the future. The assembled company was then entertained with what was described as 'a pleasant programme of suitable songs and readings' and although the audiences were apt to consist of mothers and sisters, rather than of male relations, the ladies were said to display 'no want of enthusiasm'.

Women

Although the sexes were rigorously segregated on Sundays, there never had been sex discrimination regarding learning. Females had always attended the reading and writing classes and had had access to other evening classes and to the library, and they had become members of the Lit. Its women's section had been formed in 1871 with reduced subscriptions (in 1888 one shilling compared with half as much again for males); and a dramatic section was introduced in 1881. Women therefore became eligible to take part in the productions of, for example, *'She Stoops to Conquer'* in 1889. Towards the end of the nineteenth century the men's class suggested the formation of a women's class to interest their wives. That this innovation was appreciated is evident, its aim being to provide

> 'social enjoyment and not confined to members...We should like all wives...to join us. Our meetings are a most pleasant break in the monotony of our lives'.[19]

Their programme included medical hints and sewing; visiting lecturers from the Manchester School of Domestic Economy gave talks on hygiene and cookery, and occasionally they had a recreational evening such as singing. In its fourth year a gas stove was requested and the Committee of Management, after initially demurring at the costs involved in the necessary re-lining and the new metre, granted the request.

Also, and perhaps very importantly especially during the earlier years of the nineteenth century, females were eligible to join and to benefit from the various welfare societies. Women with musical skills had always taken part in the concerts and later were appointed as organists. From an early time they had been promoted to teacher status providing basic religious and secular instruction; they visited their scholars at home in times of trouble, sickness or absence and could exert a considerable influence in this pastoral role. At this period female teachers often retired on marriage and were presented with a Bible but the 'maiden ladies who have done so much for the school [and] have received but small recognition' soldiered on, often for their lifetime.

The mother of the artist LS Lowry was organist in one of the ladies' rooms in the 1890s and Lowry was seven years old when he was first taken to Bennett Street. He was apparently too shy to stay in the boys' room where strictly speaking he should have been, but was allowed to go into the No 4 ladies room with his mother, 'hiding behind her skirts' if anyone spoke to him while she played the organ for the hymn singing. There is no evidence that Lowry attended the school regularly as his young cousins did but he maintained his interest and support to the end of his days.[20]

It was during the late nineteenth century that sport and outdoor activities became more readily accessible in the community at large and the Bennett Street committee sanctioned clubs within the school in order not to lose their young men. By the 1880s gymnastics (held at Every Street in Ancoats), swimming (held at the Osborne Street baths), cricket, football, cycling and rambling all had their place in the Bennett Street social scene.

As the nineteenth century drew to a close Bennett Street Sunday School could look back on almost one hundred years of philanthropic work in the areas of New Cross and Ancoats and they looked forward to celebrating the school's centenary in 1901.

Bennett Street Sunday School from Bennett Street

(Taken from Manchester Faces and Places in Manchester Central Library)

Above: The new church of St Paul on Oldham Road (1970 Photograph)
when the Samaritans used part of the building.

Below: New Cross Oldham Road at the end of the nineteenth century.
Note the horse omnibuses, a barefoot newsboy, and
a horse trough in the middle of the road.

Above: Silver tea service presented to David Stott, 1833
(photograph by Manchester Cathedral)

Below: David Stott's grave, in St Mary's churchyard, Bowdon

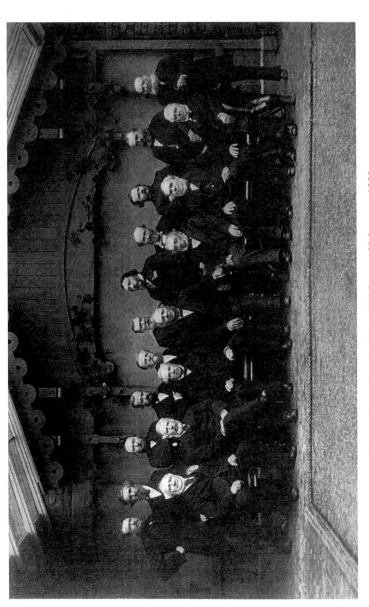

Bennett Street Sunday School Visitors and Managers 1880

Thos Philips, Peter Young, Thos Sands, W H Jordan, Robt Topham, Wm Bamford, Geo Milner, Jno Farrer, Wm Sterling, Geo Anderton, Wm Quinn,
Thos Cowle,   Jno Grantham,   Saml Goodwin,   Wm Rostron,   Chas Millward,   Thos Wm Whittaker,   Wm Morton.

(Taken from School archive in Manchester Central Library)

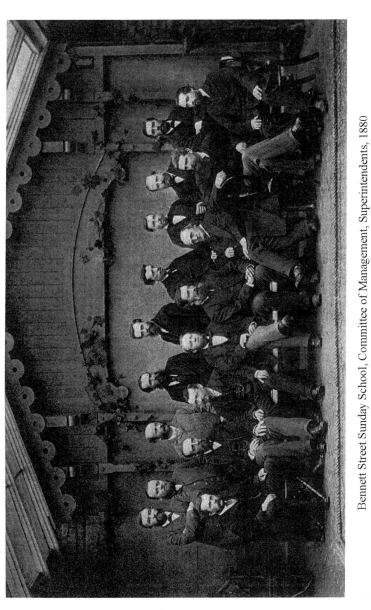

Bennett Street Sunday School, Committee of Management, Superintendents, 1880

Mark Richards, W H Grimes, H S Bamber, T Derby, J W Crossley, G Thorp, G R Hope, Jno Richards, B Gordon, A Wilkinson, Wm Crossley, Wm Thorp, Jno Peers, Wm Hoyle, Wm Lawton, B A Rediem, J Ogden.

(Taken from School archive in Manchester Central Library)

Above: Queen Victoria's Jubilee,
Bennett Street's
commemoration mug: 1897

Left: The 1897 Quiver Medal
(Manchester Central Library)

Below: Robert Raikes 150th
Anniversary medal: 1930

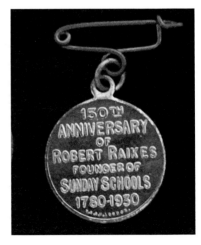

Third Jubilee of Sunday Schools 1930. Note the arrival of women on to the Committee of Management
G Luckman,   Mrs Richardson,   J Baines,   J Holmes,   G H Flint,
W Ramsden, F Fenn, H Taylor, J W Crossley, F W Wallworth, J E Chatfield, J E Bancroft, B A Redfern Jnr
G W Thompson, W R Jordan, Alfred Ogden, Rev T Owrid BA, Wm Ashton, Miss E Thomason, Albert Jordan, A T Cayton,
John R Bamford,   H Thorp,   A G Potter,   W Lees

(Taken from School archive in Manchester Central Library)

Whit Saturday 1930, '17 not out',
St Paul's cricket club v the rest of
school.

Left to right:
William Ashton
(school secretary and umpire),
Marjorie Jepson (hockey team),
Joe Ingham (cricket team).

Below: Hockey team (1930s) Left to right: Ada Newton, (?) Annie
Jepson, (?) (?) Flo Sharples, Marjorie Jepson, Hettie Thorp,
Dorothy Tonge, Kathleen Shepherd, Lilah Harrap (goal keeper).

Above: Scouts and guides (1950s) marching out of Bennett Street,
the school in the background.
(Taken from Ann Crouch collection)

Below: 1952 Mrs N D Raynor hands over the 1846 tapestry of
the school to the secretary of trustees, R D Fletcher, with
J E Bancroft and H Thorp, both of whom were trustees
(Taken from the Manchester Evening News)

Whit Monday Walks

Edwardian Whit Monday Walks
Ladies Class

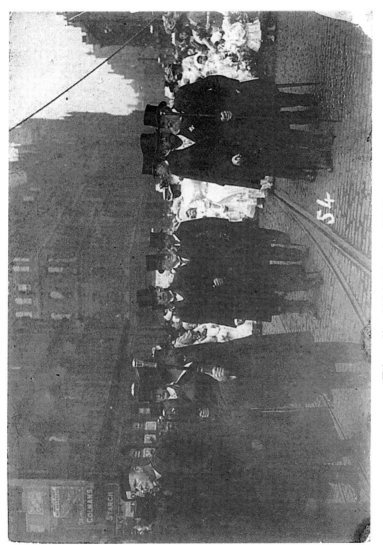

Edwardian Whit Monday Walks
Rector and church wardens

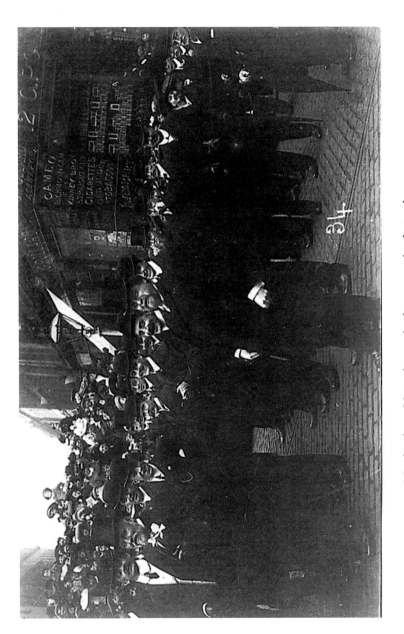

Men's class. Note the on-lookers on raised stands

Whit Monday 1920s; turning out of Princess Street.
Note the floral identification SSS (the B having walked out of the picture.)
The marshals include Mr A T Cayton front, and Mr W Lees, centre.

(Allied Newspapers)

Post-war Whit Monday 1940s in Albert Square.
Adults on the left include Elsie Cox, Muriel Luckman; on the right Ruth Taylor, Alice Cummings.
Children include Ann Cox, Greta Fletcher, Enid Cox, David Chadwick, Margaret Fletcher.

(Kemsley Newspapers)

Whit Monday 1950s on Market Street. Adults include Joyce Watson, Marie Cann. *(Published in Manchester Memories by Chris Makepeace.)*

Whit Monday 1950s in Albert Square; Diana Timperley.

(Manchester Evening News)

6

1900-1914

The Centenary of the School

It has been noted that 'On New Year's Day 1900 the British were still Victorians' and although better off than their parents' generation, generally they remained poorly nourished. Public transport in towns was well established but still horse-drawn, with tram cars developing a decade later. Cars were a luxury.

After a reign of sixty-three years, the death of Queen Victoria, at 6.30pm on Tuesday 22 January 1901 'should be regarded as the most notable occurrence' of that year. The news was brought to Bennett Street's Committee of Management whilst it was in session; the meeting was immediately adjourned and the event recorded on a blank half-page in the minute book. Edward VII came to the throne and he was succeeded by George V in 1910. Overseas exploration expanded and increasingly included expeditions to the polar regions; men also journeyed overseas to fight in the Boer War (1899-1902). At home the Women's Suffrage Movement became more aggressive in 1906; the Scout Movement was founded in 1907 and the Shops Act of 1911 entitled employees to a half-day holiday each week.[1]

Manchester achieved an open space in Piccadilly by the removal of the Royal Infirmary to a site on Oxford Road; the area adjacent to the

Cathedral housed the provision merchants dependent on the trading within the Corn Exchange, and Lewis's store was becoming a centre for the new mass retail trade.[2]

The area around Bennett Street increasingly became industrialised rather than residential as the inhabitants continued to rent or buy better property further out of the city. The most successful school members now lived in suburbs along the railway line, such as Timperley, Altrincham and Bowdon and some, but not all, although maintaining their interest and financial support, attended less regularly. Not only had the school's neighbourhood changed but the concept of the Sunday school being the 'sole available means of education and of general social intercourse and recreation' had gone for ever.

So as the twentieth century opened Bennett Street minds were concentrated on two topics: the decline in membership (for the situation was said to be 'the reverse of encouraging') and more cheerfully on the school's centenary celebrations.

The centenary of the foundation was celebrated in 1901 with three special services in church on Sunday 8 September, a date chosen to coincide with Founder's Day, followed by a week of celebration when each room held its own tea meeting with appropriate speeches. A special centenary public meeting was held (for space reasons) in the Central Hall on Oldham Street on 11 September, the addresses on this occasion being given by the Lord Mayor, the Rural Dean, the Rector and George Milner. Long service awards were presented and the company was entertained with music from the Orpheus Glee Club. The central focus of the celebration however was the leaders' announcement of their intention to publish an up-dated history of the school along with a further series of memorials and, most importantly, to extend and renovate the now antiquated building.

The Building

A centenary appeal with a target of £3,500 was launched and reported in the Manchester press; six months later this fund had reached £2,000 simply from staff and scholars. Initially reverting to their abandoned plans of 1889 architects were again consulted but it was decided that further plans should be commissioned. The new plans involved a budget of £4,000 and were robustly challenged by several members of the Committee of Management who contended that the day school's needs were being considered ahead of those of the Sunday school. Much argument ensued and after some months plans for a less grandiose scheme at about half the original estimate were finally accepted by the trustees. A new four storey wing was to be added to the school, providing a gymnasium and extra classrooms, and the space for a large hall was to be found by a reorganisation of the existing ground floor space. All this was to be achieved without the purchase of any extra land. New heating, ventilation and sanitary fittings were to be installed and the whole school wired for the new electric lighting. The extension project, originally conceived in the late 1880s, was finally brought to fruition in 1904 against a back-ground of declining numbers. The new 'Hoyle Wing' was named in recognition of Mrs Hoyle's donation of £1,000 to the building fund in memory of her husband, a former manager.[3]

*

By the start of the twentieth century the neighbourhood surrounding Bennett Street was considered to be much healthier than one hundred, or even fifty years, previously and certainly during this period the deaths of scholars were not recorded in detail although premature death continued to be an ever-present occurrence. On the death of a manager or teacher it remained the custom to drape the desk in the deceased's room with black material and to issue mourning cards. In addition, on the death of a leader, announcements were placed in the press suggesting that a 'touch of black' should be worn during the following Whit Monday procession. The females wore a black arm band and the males either a black armband or hat band. This applied to all who walked, regardless of age. Bennett Street deaths recorded in 1900 included two women teachers aged 22 and 24 and also, perhaps to be expected, one of the several members of the men's class who had 'gone forth to fight' in the Boer War. The latter would have received the Bibles and gifts sent the previous Christmas from the school via its Benevolent Committee. There was also the sad report that a scholar was 'killed in bed from a gale' in 1903 and that another was lost at sea while serving in the navy in 1905.

Throughout the 1890s Sunday attendance had been falling – from 1,564 in 1890 to 1,419 in 1898; numbers rallied in 1900 to 1,543 most probably due to the centenary celebrations. By 1904 there were 1,323 on the roll and the decline during the following decade was rapid. The figure dropped below 1,000 for the first time in 1908 and by 1914 was 861.

Because of an accident in school involving an outside workman, the leaders were moved to insure scholars against accidents; the day scholars at 2s 6d per 100 and the Sunday scholars at sixpence per 100. The day school was transferred to the local authority in 1903. (See Chapter 9, page 155 on the day school.)

Anniversary Sunday

In spite of the falling numbers, the anniversary collections continued to achieve around £300. In 1904 it was recorded that this figure included donations from former members and friends in every part of England and even from America, Australia and India, and that many were accompanied by letters 'expressing in the warmest terms continued affection for the old place'. Fund raising followed the national pattern of jumble sales, bazaars and sales of work; and a pet and flower show was also held in a gallant 'attempt to promote window gardening in the district'.

Religion

The decline in numbers was particularly noticeable in the older classes; teachers were said to have become lax in both their timekeeping and the preparation of their lessons; a new rule of two teachers to a class was introduced and an accommodation reached regarding travelling difficulties and the resultant problems with timekeeping. The Visitors were asked to make unannounced appearances and, in order to provide variety, an interchange of desks (or exchange of pulpits) was introduced.

The older boys were introduced to a new syllabus working towards the diocesan scripture examinations; the men's select class chose to read the *Life of St Paul* and, in a new venture, took turns to deliver the address at the full church services now being held monthly in each of the rooms. The school's Tract Society still functioned and the British and Foreign Bible Society, on the occasion of their own centenary offered to provide the school with new large Bibles for the desk in each room in return for a sermon being preached and a collection made. This offer was accepted.

The Lit

Although its numbers had declined from the 200 members of the 1870s/80s, the Literary Society remained active and innovative; for instance in 1908 it started an economics class and at the opening conversazione of the session when a resumé of the society's work was given by the president, it had become customary to invite a distinguished person to deliver an address and distribute the prizes. The range of topics covered can be illustrated by quoting one or two examples from a four week period in February/March 1904 when the programme included: a popular night comprising readings from Tennyson's longer poems, scenes from Sheridan's *The Rivals* and Shakespeare's *Henry VIII*, and the reading of a Sheridan farce, *'St Patrick's Day or the Scheming Lieutenant'*. Papers were given on walks around the town and on Samuel Pepys and a separate meeting was devoted annually to a critique and readings from the newly delivered *Odds and Ends*. On one evening a paper on John Locke (1632-1704) formed the first part of the proceedings 'with the rest of the evening being given up to a frolic'. This latter event was subsequently reported in the school magazine as follows under the heading of 'The adjourned Parliamentary Debate':

'...happily for the evening's enjoyment, the estimable members who were supposed to represent Parliamentary Divisions were in a jovial mood, and consequently much amusement was created. The contest might be spoken of in times to come as "The Battle of the Hats," as in imitation of Parliamentary procedure the members when rising to speak clapped a hat upon their heads. Each side made use of only one hat, the side representing the Government passing about from speaker to speaker an ordinary hard felt hat [a bowler], whilst the Opposition looked extremely funny in a soft felt trilby hat. These two hats were in constant requisition as members interrupted speeches in a manner which, outside the

Parliamentary arena, would be curtly referred to as "rude"; points of order were called for every minute, and each time the hat was snatched up and fixed on the head in a most undignified fashion. In fact the poor hard felt and the poor trilby had no peace. It is not easy to say which had the more ludicrous effect. The hard felt could not be stretched, and when it was placed on an unusually large cranium it gave the speaker a jaunty careless air, and besides it had a tendency to wobble about with each movement of the head. But when it descended upon a skull of limited dimensions then did the audience roar beyond all bounds, for the speech seemed to issue in deep sepulchral tones from under the funereal head-gear. The other Section contributed its share to the fun for, although the hat it possessed was flexible enough to sit properly on any shape or size of head, except those particularly diminutive or enlarged, yet by throwing up the crown or turning down the rim, some very grotesque figures were cut by the members of the Opposition. The evening was an excellent one for sport. Good jokes and good humour abounded and, though the debate suffered, it was agreed at the finish that a finer frolic never had been.'[4]

Whit Week

To commemorate the school centenary a new banner was commissioned for the Whit Monday procession in 1901; medals and centenary ribbons were worn and past members were invited to take part. The Manchester Anglican Walks celebrated their own centenary that year and seventy-six Bennett Street scholars (thirty-eight boys and thirty-eight girls) were invited to a special Walks centenary service in the Cathedral.[5]

The new Bennett Street banner of royal blue with gold and cream lettering, within a framework of stylised flowers, (see photograph on page 106) declared that they were:

'ST PAUL'S
BENNETT STREET
SUNDAY SCHOOLS
DAVID STOTT
FOUNDER'

Schools with special anniversaries walked near to the head of the
procession always led by the Cathedral contingent and formed part of
the Cathedral congregation for the service. It followed that the nearer
a school was to the head of the procession, the earlier it had to leave
school.

By the early twentieth century specially chartered buses, trams and
trolley buses had joined with the railway as modes of transport for the
Whit Week excursions. The 1905 programme records that on Whit
Monday afternoon 140 teachers and adults journeyed to Bramhall; 700
scholars and friends were transported to the Wednesday sports at
Davenport where eccles cakes replaced the usual buns as the
children's treat; and the following day a 'goodly number had travelled
to their destination by corporation tram' but it was noted that the adult
train trip to Keswick had required them to 'rise so unusually early'.
Once again, the Bennett Street child's opinion of early rising differs
somewhat (albeit written some twenty years previously):

> 'The one fact we desired to ascertain was, at what time we were,
> along with teachers, to assemble in school on this particular
> morning. If the time was early enough, say half-past four or
> five o'clock, there was a hum expressive of the greatest possible
> contentment...'.[6]

Social Activities

Although the Orpheus Glee Club was now giving regular and much appreciated contributions to parties and concerts, it was at this juncture that the Committee of Management found it necessary to stipulate that there be 'no objectionable items in the entertainment' specifically at the New Year parties, as the arrangements had begun to change from the long-established concert format. In 1900 a short play, written within the school, was presented; it concerned a 'Mrs Marmalade' who was said to be 'well preserved'. The following year, while the new Education Bill was progressing through Parliament (passed in 1902), the entertainers were preparing an educational burlesque. The result was *'Widow Girton's Academy for Young Gentlemen'*, the widow being played by a male (a 'dame'). (Girton College Cambridge, founded in 1869, was for women only. This gives some insight into the intellectual level of humour displayed.) The programme announced that 'This Academy is conducted in accordance with the New Education Bill. Canes of the finest quality only used'. In 1904 they presented *Robinson Crusoe,* the programme for which included a note that 'The HORDIENCE is requested not to blow out the footlights'. In 1905 they staged the *Trial of Bardell and Pickwick* and in 1908 produced their first full length pantomime.[7]

The summer social scene was increasingly active. In addition to tea parties, each class and society had their summer outing, usually of a ramble followed by a tea. In 1905 the Lit's summer outing took place at the end of May with an age range present of between three years and eighty. After an 'invigorating walk' from Altrincham to Millington they had tea in the open air and admired the spread of bluebells on the hillside. Those 'too young or too old to walk' rode by wagonette. These Lit picnics were obviously eagerly anticipated as the writer records how they 'long[ed] for the time when once more we shall leave our humdrum life behind and again for a few hours commune with nature'. The men's class rambling club travelled to Roaches via Ashton-under-Lyne and Cock Brook, and considered it 'the most picturesque tram route ever taken'; they felt it a 'pity the people of Manchester know so little of the beauties within ten or twelve miles of where they live'. That same year the sewing class travelled to Blackpool which, since their last visit, 'now possesses a prom about three miles long' where most of the space had been 'taken from the sea'. This sewing class, which included young women from the parish in addition to school members, was said to be for 'mild recreation' whereas the women's class was reported to be 'more ambitious'. By 1911 the sewing class had been disbanded and a Girls' Friendly Society introduced.[8]

A (new) young men's social club for those over sixteen offered exercise, chess, draughts and senior billiards and also provided a good supply of magazines and papers; the Committee of Management vetted their choice of organised games. In 1912 the boy scouts are mentioned for the first time but it was the swimming club which took the first steps towards female emancipation in the school by decreeing that in appointing their club committee 'two shall be ladies'.

So although the 'social side proceeded apace with vigour and success', the leaders did find the state of Sunday attendance to be 'deplorable', and in 1912 admitted their concerns in public. The Manchester Diocese Sunday School Committee however gave their opinion that 'in recent years there has been a great improvement in Sunday school methods...the number in attendance has increased'; but in response the Committee of Management wrote that 'no ripple of such a tide has reached the shores of Bennett Street'. At their meeting in July 1914 they announced that they were determined to 'make an effort and carry on'.

But one month later the country was at war and everything changed.

7

1914-1918

The First World War

The First World War was declared in August 1914, but in the preceding months the government's concerns had also included Irish Home Rule and the activities of the Suffragette Movement.

Manchester continued a much healthier city with an extended infrastructure of water, gas and electricity supplies and improvements to housing. The cotton industry was at its peak and wages had made a real advance. The city now had a wide-ranging choice of educational establishments including the School of Art where L S Lowry was enrolled, the Technical School to which Bennett Street sent its Grantham scholarship boys, and that for domestic economy which supplied the school with occasional lecturers. It is recorded that 'in 1914 an average working class family spent three quarters of its income on food and housing'; its leisure activities now included, for instance, attendance at football matches or the music hall and shopping, with Lewis's store in the forefront for the less wealthy classes.[1]

At Bennett Street the most significant events of this period were the death of George Milner and the centenary of the school building in 1918. On Christmas Day 1914 George Milner died aged 85. He had been a member of the school almost all his life. A key figure in its management for many years, his twin passions of self-education generally and the English language in particular had influenced the direction of Bennett Street's adult education for decades, and it is his writings which give insight into the work of the school during the nineteenth century. He was also a great Mancunian and his obituaries in the Manchester press were long and detailed. An appreciation of Milner is printed at the end of this chapter.

Religion

For the first six months of 1914 the energies of the Bennett Street Committee of Management were exercised with what they considered 'the deplorable state of the attendance on Sundays'. In 1913 there were 947 scholars on the rolls compared with 1,543 in 1899 and there was a general recognition among the leaders that 'times [are] different from those 50 years ago'. Demolition of housing in the New Cross area meant that the local population was moving further away from the school and it was also thought that parents were less anxious to provide religious education for their children. However the rector, Rev D E Walker, questioned whether the Sunday school services were sufficiently attractive. The committee agreed that they must modernise, although they harboured a suspicion that 'amusements had a great deal to do with it' since brass bands now played in the parks on Sundays. Yet again the 'unattractiveness of our school' was cited as a possible deterrent to attendance.

Action was taken. The Sunday services became more varied; psalms were shortened, canticles introduced and special musical services arranged. Instruction classes for the teachers were re-started, as were their quarterly meetings, and a new list of graded lessons was introduced. The visiting of absentee scholars by teachers was to be carried out systematically during the week and teachers were requested to attend church more regularly; scholars' church attendance was reorganised. The committee remained most emphatic that teachers should not be press-ganged, much preferring willing, but able, volunteers. In short, a general tightening up of procedures took place. There is no evidence of the effectiveness – or otherwise – of these new arrangements as after the declaration of war on 4 August 1914 the situation changed completely. Bennett Street leaders became more interested in simply 'keeping the place going' and to providing pastoral care, not just to their local community but also to their members on active service. They were agreed that 'our work must go on'.

During the initial discussions on reorganisation cessation of the morning sessions had been considered, but once war was declared it was felt that there was an increased desire for worship among all sections of the community and so both the Sunday morning and Sunday afternoon sessions were retained.

The school continued to let out rooms to selected organisations such as the Manchester and Northern Ornithological Society which held a Bird Show in 1916, and the Church Missionary Society which arranged a conference in 1917.

War-Time Conditions

The government's war-time regulations included restriction in the use of paper (the school magazine was reduced in size and waste paper was sold) and the banning of street lighting, making attendance at evening events less appealing. The Royal Flying Corps, founded in 1912, formed a new part of Britain's defences and in 1916 the Bennett Street buildings and contents were insured against damage from aircraft. In tune with the patriotic ethos prevailing, the school invested in War Loan and in 1915 agreed to lend £100 to Manchester Corporation for 5 years at an interest rate of 4½ per cent. Rising prices posed financial problems; increased taxes had been levied on tea and tobacco, and income tax had risen (it was 40 per cent up from the pre-war years). Few large subscriptions were now received but the committee was happy to report that there was a willingness 'to give as ye are able'.

By December 1914 over fifty Bennett Street men had volunteered for the forces. As the men left for active service, the ladies stepped into the breach by taking over the men's teaching duties, and the women's section of the Literary and Educational Society gave papers to the main society in order to keep it going. The number of women in paid employment rose by two million nationally in 1916 and the Bennett Street management recorded that in addition to their extra duties in school, as well as their daytime occupations and war-time evening work, the ladies could also be found 'rushing about with a handcart on dark nights' collecting for the jumble sale.

The introduction of conscription in 1916, first of single men and later of married men, meant that by 1917 there were scarcely any male teachers left in No. 2 Room. No 2 Room (older boys) and No 4 Room (older girls and ladies) were therefore combined for the morning sessions.

Women in Administration

The strain of running the school was beginning to tell on the remaining, that is mostly older, men and in February 1918, finding no male volunteers, the committee 'resolved that the secretary endeavour to get a lady collector' for the magazine advertisements. This is the first indication of women being directly involved in administration. Although previously they had been teachers and organists, they had not even figured as being in charge of catering. Following this resolution, a lady was appointed as joint-caterer for the next New Year's Eve Party; and from this time onwards female teachers were permitted to express formally their comments on Whit Week arrangements. These changes paved the way for women to be appointed to management positions in the school. The process was slow but mirrored the situation prevailing nationally where women had been appointed to positions vacated by men joining the forces, positions which had hitherto been barred to females. In July 1918, a motion was put before the school committee regarding 'admission of women to the Committee of Management' but by the September meeting it had no seconder and the matter was referred to the trustees. The trustees held a special meeting in February 1919 to 'consider the advisability of the appointment of women on the Committee of Management and also as superintendents'. Again no progress was made, but it was decided 'that a joint Meeting of Trustees and Managers be called to discuss the whole question'. This is the only record of such a joint meeting in the history of the school. The result of that joint meeting was a proposal that the teachers and room officials and also the scholars of the adult class, be invited to appoint annually two of their number to serve on the Committee of Management. This proposal was carried unanimously and at the following annual trustee meeting in June 1919 it was confirmed that the teacher representatives on the Committee of Management included four ladies, two from each of the female rooms.

Prizes

From as early as the autumn of 1914 the question of the annual distribution of prizes had become an emotive issue. Immediately after the start of the war it had been announced that the managers would forego their annual prizes but that those of the teachers would be presented as usual. These books, chosen by the recipients and presented by the Visitors each Christmas remained an annual recognition of services 'as a gratuitous teacher' but in 1915 both donors and recipients were 'unanimous for withholding this year'. The following year teachers were asked to forego their prizes but, 'all teachers or scholars who have joined the forces be given a prize this year as if they had attended school'; the Bible continued to be presented to female teachers who retired on marriage. The Grantham Scholarships to the School of Technology were also withheld until after the war.

Charity and Welfare

Despite the war the school's charitable and welfare traditions continued. Active co-operation with the Red Cross Society was encouraged and collections within the school for this society were sanctioned, a reversal of normal practice when collecting in school for outside societies was not permitted, but in this instance patriotic sentiment prevailed. In 1917 heating problems were experienced due to 'insufficient stoking' - the caretaker had died. A collection took place and from the resulting fund the committee started to pay the sum of ten shillings a week to his widow. The school founded a Comforts Fund so that Christmas cards and 'parcels of comforts' could be sent to their troops; this was financed throughout the war by jumble sales, whist drives and socials. There seems no evidence of the content of the Bennett Street parcels, but 'comforts' were generally considered to be cigarettes and tobacco, chocolate and sweets and sometimes hand-knitted articles such as scarves.

Whit Week

In 1914 the arrangements for Whit Week proceeded as normal, the start of the war still being several months distant, and in the Whit Monday procession the Bennett Street scholars wore 'a token of black' in tribute to George Milner. In 1916 the processions were initially in doubt but the civic authorities ultimately gave permission. For financial reasons Bennett Street wished to engage only one band instead of their more normal two, and were negotiating on the terms of 'if there be no procession there be no pay'; the band wanted half pay if there was no procession. However, just ten days before Whit Monday the city cancelled all arrangements for processions and festivities 'in consequence of the War and the Government and Corporation resolutions'. The Prime Minister had announced the previous week that the Whit Monday Bank Holiday would be postponed until Tuesday 8 August (the day after August Bank Holiday) as such an arrangement would 'facilitate the continuance of munitions work'. Manchester's Lord Mayor therefore rescinded the permission already given for the Whit Monday processions and Bennett Street abandoned all its Whit Week arrangements for that year. This was the first time the walks had not been held since 1801.[2]

During the following years of the war the festivities were discussed, not only against a backdrop of war, but also against one of rising prices. Day excursions were curtailed as the railway declined to offer reduced tickets; the Committee of Management decreed that if there was 'no train to be had, and failing any other means horse lorries [were] to be engaged'. Unusually, but in tune with the times, a Whit Monday afternoon visit to High Lane included a church service prior to the tea. As it had been considered too expensive to hire the usual tent for the tea, it is not clear where the tea was actually held but what is clear is that there were 'insufficient buns' and that 'the ladies who made tea...were left behind when the walk commenced'. Why this happened we do not know. Could it perhaps be that because so many men had gone to war, an inexperienced organiser was in charge? The records do not say. The customary long-distance outing on Whit Friday was curtailed to a visit to Millington in Cheshire with everyone paying their own expenses. This contrasts with the pre-war rail trips organised to the Lancashire coast, the Lake District or mid-Wales. The 1914 excursion to Rhyl was itself a less ambitious destination than previously and in 1917 and 1918 the journeys were much more local, to Prestwich and Poynton.

Social Activities

The committee agonised over whether, in time of war, it was appropriate to hold the usual parties during the Christmas season. Very early in the war it was considered, 'desirable if possible' to do so and formed its own Food Control Committee to cut out waste caused through over-catering. Throughout 1916 and 1917 certain foods were in short supply and prices consequently high; sugar, butter and tea (the staples of any Sunday school party) were affected but, until 1917, were not rationed. From 1916 onwards although the government had exhorted the public to eat less meat, actual rationing of it was not imposed until 1918. The parties did continue throughout the war with beef and ham on the menu in 1914, but as the food shortages tightened this was reduced to 'beef only' in 1916 and to a sweet tea in 1919; they had managed to have oranges in 1917.

In 1916 wartime entertainment tax was included in the price of party tickets (2d on 1s tickets, 1d on those at 7d). With the exception of the teachers' Christmas 'treat', Bennett Street parties had always been by priced ticket. This habit was waived in 1918 when the 'blue service' (the wounded) and ex-servicemen were admitted to the parties free of charge. The entertainment arrangements also changed. In 1914, a large number of the male members having joined the forces, the committee was prepared to pay for the evening entertainment. The Ideal Entertainment Company was offered '£3 10s 0d if they wore evening dress but only £2 15s 0d otherwise'.

The meetings of the school's social groups took place as usual. On the sporting side, the Cycling Club was still active at the start of the war, and the Cricket Club held its usual social, but in 1915 the Lads Club was described as 'the late Lads Club' and its billiard table sold.

Roll of Honour

The first mention of a 'Roll of Honour' occurs in November 1914. Bennett Street used this phrase to mean a list, with photographs, of those who had joined the forces. It did not mean fatalities. By December 1914 it was noted that '50-60 of our young men' had joined up. Ultimately the Roll of Honour, 'our School's contribution to uphold the honour of our country in the present war' contained 'upwards of 300 names'. These names included past scholars, although the majority were said to be active teachers, along with scholars from the adult class and the upper room of boys.

One of 'our lads', Lance Corporal Ingles, who in 1916 had written home to his parents that 'I had a nice birthday for we took some trenches', was discovered to have been awarded the Distinguished Conduct Medal (DCM) for this 'gallant deed'. His friends at the front subsequently supplied the information that he had been

'advancing with his platoon when he noticed a machine gun was working havoc among the ranks of his comrades. In spite of the hail of bullets, he dashed up to the machine gun, killed the German who was working it and captured the gun itself'.

The men's class also received a letter from someone who

'had seen a Bennett Street man at the front who was on support duty with six others when a shell fell among them, wounding four. The other two ran away but Mr Shepherd stayed with the four wounded to bandage and help them all he could. Shells continued to explode all round them.'

The class expressed itself proud that one of their number should have 'borne himself so worthily under such terrifying conditions'.[3]

The first fatalities of Bennett Street men were noted in 1915 with six deaths in Gallipoli and France, and it was resolved that a memorial tablet recording the names of those killed be placed in both school and church. Thirty-three Bennett Street men in all were killed in the Great War. Designs for two memorial tablets in metal were commissioned from Baxendale's of Manchester and an appeal for funds inaugurated. The chosen site of the school memorial was on the wall of the lecture hall platform. The unveiling ceremony, 'no meeting was ever so highly charged with emotion', took place on 23 January 1921 at 2.45 pm. The Last Post was sounded, 'O Rest in the Lord' from Mendelssohn's oratorio 'Elijah' was sung and a Benediction was given by the Rector. The tablet was unveiled by William Ashton (Secretary and Treasurer to the Trustees). The following week the tablet in church was unveiled by J E Bamford, on 30 January 1921.[4] An appreciation of William Ashton is given following the chapter on the interwar period.

---------------- * ----------------

When the war ended scholar numbers had reduced once more. Not only had there been the steady stream of men leaving to fight, but there had also been a decrease in female attendance, attributed variously to street lighting restrictions and the absence of young men in the school. The women who remained seized their opportunity to take part in the running of the school, and this was never relinquished.

Nationally the church was wrestling with an unaccustomed dilemma; how to preach to a people suffering from the horrors of the war, people who were increasingly sceptical about the concept of a God of Love. Bennett Street faced this problem too and, as in similar inner city institutions, their numbers were never to recover.

GEORGE MILNER (1829 – 1914)

It is largely George Milner's writings which have made the history of Bennett Street's first one hundred years available to us today, adding detail to the bald facts in the minute books.

Once described as 'Bennett Street incarnate' George Milner was connected with the school for eighty-two years as scholar, teacher, manager, Visitor, trustee, committee man, publicist and chronicler. He was very much a 'Manchester Man', eventually being made a Freeman of the City in 1905.

He was born in the Bennett Street area and lived in very humble circumstances, his father (also George) dying whilst he was still an infant. He himself wrote that his first attendance at Bennett Street was at such an early age that his 'legs [were] as yet unembarrassed by trousers' and he was placed in the girls' room to be cared for. These were the days when little boys wore skirts until they were ceremoniously put into breeches, or 'breeched', around the age of four or five.

He attended day school at the local Lancasterian School and started his working life serving in a book shop on Market Street He did not stay there long but the love of books never left him. For the rest of his life he was passionately interested in literature, wrote both poetry and prose and developed a love of nature and the countryside. He found work in the Manchester cotton trade

Bennett Street Sunday School 1801-1966

in a grey cloth company with premises on Mosley Street next to the Portico Library, and rose to a position requiring him to stand on the Royal (Cotton) Exchange. He was however said to be 'singularly unworldly'. The rector, Rev D E Walker, considered him the most guileless of men, but remarked on his kindness, sympathy and courteous encouragement. Others variously described him as cultured, an unhurried man of order and method and as being at home in any company. At Bennett Street he was a towering presence both literally and metaphorically; the photograph of the Visitors in 1880 shows him standing head and shoulders above his colleagues and, with his full beard, bearing more than a passing resemblance to the poet Tennyson whose work he so greatly admired.

It was Milner's belief that a Sunday school should be a place not only for imparting religious teaching but should serve also as a social agency and a college for the working class. His own wish was that Bennett Street should provide elementary education, culture of the higher kind, especially leaning towards English literature, philanthropy (although he did not care for the word) and both indoor and outdoor recreation.

He was not a wealthy man, his monetary contributions were modest for 'he had not the means'; indeed his legacy to Bennett Street was never paid out, 'there was no money'. But in his lifetime he was able to indulge in travel to areas such as the Lake District, North Wales, Scotland and Ireland. He enjoyed mountain-climbing holidays and his love of the countryside in general was great, as was his passion for recording it in his writings, paintings and sketches.

Milner loved the English language and its literature. He taught for many years in Bennett Street's evening classes; one of his obituaries describes him as a teacher 'gifted to the point of genius' and a former student recalled him encouraging them to try their hand at writing and introducing them to new books or to cheap editions of the classics. He was one of the three founders of the Bennett Street Literary and Educational Society and the editor of their Odds and Ends Manuscript Magazine, retiring in 1905 after fifty years in the post, although he continued to be a constant and talented contributor both in words and by means of his water colour sketches. No Bennett Street event was complete without him as speaker. His enthusiasm for literature and for the countryside had a direct influence on the adult curriculum in Bennett Street and on the introduction of rambles and picnics into their summer programmes.

In the city itself it was said that it was hard to imagine Manchester without him. He contributed articles to many local journals and was considered the doyen of the city's literary life, the last of the Lancashire group of poets that had included Waugh, Brierley and Laycock. At a dinner to celebrate his twenty-five years as president of the Manchester Literary Club the programme included songs for which he had written the words. For some of his writing he used the pen name of Geoffrey Melbrook.

He was also a magistrate and served on many of Manchester's educational and cultural committees. He became chairman of the Manchester City News and was a Warden of the Cathedral; one of his obituaries speaks of his 'work in connection with protracted architectural work of restoring the edifice as we know it today'.

His last years brought many problems and sufferings. His wife, having borne him seven children, died in 1895. In 1900 his right arm was amputated following a gun accident while on holiday in Ireland, but he recovered from this trauma and taught himself to write again, and to paint, with his left hand. He took to wearing a cloak rather than a coat and also sported a wide brimmed hat. This mode of dress accentuated his Tennysonian appearance for he did not lose his hair; it turned white and in old age he was described as having a leonine head and the appearance of a patriarch. He became deaf, and on what was to be his final Whit Monday procession (1914) he was driven through the streets as he had become too infirm to walk.

But honours too came to him in old age; an Honorary MA was conferred on him by the University of Manchester and in 1905 he was made an Honorary Freeman of the City. The Silver Casket presented to him on that occasion bore pictures of the Town Hall and the Cathedral and, on the reverse side, the façade of Bennett Street Sunday School and of St Paul's Church.[5]

George Milner died on Christmas Day 1914 and is buried in the churchyard of St Mary's Church, Bowdon within yards of David Stott's grave. His funeral service was taken by the rector of St Paul's New Cross, and was attended by the Lord Mayor, the Town Clerk and the Dean of the Cathedral. Representatives of the city magistrates and of the literary and arts associations with which he had been connected were also present. Twelve named men from Bennett Street attended and, more unusually for the time, 'a number of ladies all long and intimately associated with the School'.[6]

Following George Milner's death no other Bennett Street member took up the task of recording the work of the school other than through the formal minute books.

George Milner appears on the 1880 photograph of the Visitors and Managers.

8

1918-1939

The Interwar Years

The declaration of the Armistice at the end of the First World War - on the eleventh hour of the eleventh day of the eleventh month of 1918 - brought feelings of immense thankfulness to the whole nation and ushered in a decade when women were finally given the vote on a par with men (1928) and when they shortened their skirts and flattened their chests. The male fashion statement of the time was Oxford bags. Both males and females listened to the new jazz music and danced the Charleston. But in contrast to the frivolity, all were affected by the General Strike in 1926 and the threat of unemployment, which for many became a personal reality. Financially, the great depression of the early 1930s followed the Wall Street crash of 1929. The economic situation revived in the mid-1930s when a great deal of low cost modern housing was built nationally. [1] The final years of the decade were once more over-shadowed by the threat - and then the grim reality - of the Second World War.

No indication has been found that Bennett Street celebrated King George V's silver jubilee in 1935 or commemorated his death in 1936. The minutes are similarly silent about the abdication of Edward VIII at the end of that year and the Coronation of George VI in 1937. These silences are in marked contrast to the reactions to Queen Victoria's jubilees and they open debate on the change in attitudes and the influence of the Great War.

In Manchester

'[In the 1930s]...The highest unemployment figures and the worst housing conditions prevailed in the inner residential ring, in the districts of Miles Platting, Chorlton-on-Medlock, Hulme, Ancoats, Angel Meadow and Redbank'.[2]

New Cross does not figure on this list but is adjacent to the areas mentioned. With much of the cottage property having been demolished 'warehouses, a railway goods station and a petrol station (which the leaders noted was a sign of the times) enclose[d] the school' and Thompson Street was transformed into a broader highway. In the city centre Manchester's round Central Reference Library in St Peter's Square was opened in 1934.

As it was no longer a residential parish the closure and demolition of St Paul's church was mooted in April 1927. Public meetings which 'brought a large gathering of present and past worshippers at St Paul's, and many old and new Bennett Streeters together' were held and deputations met with the Bishop. The eventual outcome was that St Paul's was not demolished but its parish combined with that of St Michael of Angel Meadow and St Thomas of Red Bank, St Paul's being the parish church.

One hundred and fifty years of the Sunday School Movement was celebrated nationally in 1930. As their commemoration Bennett Street held a special jubilee social evening when the address was the 'Origin of Sunday Schools and of Bennett Street'. An official photograph of the managers was commissioned, a free party for the children arranged and all were presented with commemorative medals. The school also attended the local rally held in the Albert Hall on Peter Street. Further national celebrations to recognise '400 years since the Bible was set up in our churches', took place in 1938 with the school organising the rare event of a combined meeting of all scholars with the men's class; the latter continued to flourish and had celebrated its own jubilee in 1920.

During the interwar period Bennett Street's own special events included welcoming home their troops and the marking of the centenary of the building, celebrations for which continued throughout the year 1918/1919. Immediately after the Armistice an influenza epidemic swept through the country and the city but although closure of the school was considered briefly the celebrations continued with a social gathering when the Roll of Honour was displayed. Founder's Day that year was attended by the Lord Mayor, an indication of the importance attached to the centenary as a civic presence in Bennett Street was a rare occurrence. There was still no meat at the tea parties (and in 1922 no meal at all) but entertainment continued with music, addresses and the presentation of long-service testimonials and diocesan medals. For this special year there was also an exhibition of 'old prizes, cups, and medals'; refreshments were available, admission was free and illustrated souvenir programmes were sold at 3d. The New Year festivities were extended to include a pageant illustrating costumes from the previous one hundred years.

The troops returned gradually and the official welcome home for all 'returned soldiers, sailors and airmen' took place in February 1920. Two free tickets were presented to each returning serviceman 'for self and lady' and were also sent to parents and widows of deceased members. Ordinary members of the school were charged elevenpence ha'penny and managers' tickets were one shilling. The event took the form of a social evening, the musical items being performed by the current members and with the drawings for the proposed war memorial tablets on display. And what did these returning troops find? Many of them returned to find they had no job (there were one million unemployed in the country) and, of particular relevance in Manchester, that the decline of the Lancashire cotton industry was increasingly evident. The school's employment registry continued to assist in finding positions for members who were unemployed.

The post-war atmosphere at Bennett Street, as in the whole Sunday School Movement, indeed in the whole country, had undergone a change:

> 'Lads who left, [to serve in the war] return as grown men with dreadful memories of their experiences...and find No.2 classes inappropriate' but...a warm welcome awaits [them] in the Men's Class and at church'.[3]

In 1919 because of the returnees, the numbers attending school increased, but compared with pre-war were sadly depleted. In 1914 there had been 861 scholars on the roll and 106 teachers, whereas in 1919 there were 649 scholars and 86 teachers. The four rooms were still in operation, plus the men's class and the select class, but by 1923 numbers had decreased to the extent that it was suggested, but not implemented, that the two rooms of older scholars be closed for the morning session.

The committee noted that while serving in the forces troops had been playing games on a Sunday, indeed only on a Sunday. The Sunday Games Bill was before parliament and allowed organised sport to be played on a Sunday afternoon. The passing of such a Bill, while not necessarily affecting church services because of their timing, would be 'disastrous to Sunday Schools'. Additional concerns were that people were choosing to spend Sunday afternoons 'in the country', and also that entertainment was slowly becoming available in the home via the wireless. But the leaders concurred with the view expressed by Canon Peter Green in 1924 that 'the Sunday School [Movement] was extraordinarily valuable to the nation'.

The Building

Because of the presence of the day school the maintenance of the building continued to be shared with the Manchester Education Committee (MEC) but the lecture hall which was not used by the day school was the sole responsibility of the Sunday school. The 1920s/30s was a growth period in the school's social work with the lecture hall at its centre; improvements to this room were therefore necessary. The platform was extended and hung with new curtains; a fire extinguisher and an ambulance box were installed, ventilation was improved and an emergency exit constructed. After complaints of 'tampering' by persons unknown, the fuse-box was overhauled and new electric switches were installed on the stairs 'so that they can be lit up without going to the caretaker's [house]'. In one of the seemingly rare efforts at 'beautifying', shades were purchased for the hall's bare bulbs. The 1898 ban on smoking having been relaxed at some point, a proposal in 1922 that there be no smoking in the building on a Sunday was not carried, demonstrating a considerable difference in public attitude compared with the early twenty-first century. The state of the hall's flooring caused concern in 1929 and a school member undertook to 'take all the knots off'. This may not have been totally successful as in 1931 a polished dance floor was laid, an amenity not normally associated with a Sunday school, but an indication that at some point dancing had been sanctioned at the social evenings.

Other post-war refurbishment included a 'slow combustion stove' for the ladies' room; other rooms received new matting, all pictures were inspected and cords repaired. The organs were overhauled and in 1923 a new instrument was purchased for the men's class, to which the class itself contributed £25.

Decoration was the province of the MEC. In January 1924 they requested closure of the building for this purpose; the Committee of Management would not agree to total closure but did agree to close the required rooms for two weeks in July and to re-organise the Sunday and evening activities. The minutes record that on the first Sunday of the intended closure the school held their service in church, following which the committee held an emergency meeting 'at the church door' resolving that 'in the event of the decorators not having started work [the following day] we carry on as usual at School'. It was not until July in the following year (1925) that the decorators moved in.

Administration

Paper had been in short supply during the war, resulting in early post-war requisitions for library books, large-type hymn books and four dozen of the school's own small hymn books. In 1923 the purchase of prayer books was deferred as 'there would possibly be an alteration in the new prayer book'. The new Book of Common Prayer was published in 1928. One of the alterations in the wording was that in the marriage service the bride did not promise to obey her husband. The viability of the school magazine caused concern throughout the interwar period. It was running at a loss and several new editors were successively appointed. Some obviously thought that its usefulness had run its course, as in 1920 a 'decision on retaining the magazine ought to be taken by the Committee in general'. So although 'reconsider in six months' became a recurrent phrase in the minutes, the magazine did continue in reduced form until the school closed.

Women

By 1919 there were four lady members on the Committee of Management 'taking a lively interest in the management of the school and doing really good work'. Although the proposal that ladies be eligible to serve as superintendents was carried in the same year, it was evidently not automatic to consider them. In 1926 difficulty was experienced in filling one of these vacancies and a formal request was made to the committee asking if they would be 'agreeable to ladies being appointed'. This request was granted; a lady superintendent was appointed in 1928 and another in 1929. More prosaically it was a lady who asked for a stop tap to be installed on the ground floor 'so that the water could easily be turned off'.

Prizes

The re-introduction of teachers' prizes, withdrawn during the war, was considered in 1923 but was not implemented. A new prize however was given to scholars for knowledge of (i.e. reciting) forty of the prayer-book's collects. Regret was once more voiced that it was only now and again that people competed for the music prizes. The recognition of 50 years' service by teachers and managers continued, the customary portraits being replaced by the more modern photograph. In 1934 the committee decreed there was no room for further photographs on the walls and the testimonial would continue in book form; in 1935 it was 'a book and a purse of five guineas'.

Scouts

Considering the numbers involved, remarkably few complaints about scholar behaviour prior to the war are recorded, but in 1922 it was felt necessary to prohibit 'loitering on landing, stairs and corridors' and on one Sunday in 1923 No 1 small room had been found to be 'full of scouts' when they ought to have been in their classes. Permission had been granted in 1919 for the formation of a scout troop under the leadership of one of the school's wounded soldiers. The troop drew most of its boys from the inner city area, and an element took time to settle into the discipline of the troop and the Sunday school. A sympathetic but firm approach by scout leaders and Sunday school leaders eventually brought about better behaviour.[4]

The troop wore a uniform of grey shirts, blue shorts and white neckerchiefs and each paid a contribution of one ha'penny per week. A special service was held in church, during Sunday school time, to consecrate the troop colour and the older girls, as well as the boys who were not scouts, were permitted to attend; church parade became a twice monthly feature of Sunday morning service. When the troop had been operating for a few months the school loaned them the sum of £20 to buy bugles and drums to form a band. The committee anticipated that they would make 'brave use' of these when they brought up the rear of the school's procession on Whit Monday. The new scout troop paved the way for a wolf cub pack and later the formation of the guides was followed by the brownies.

Anniversary Sunday

The anniversary collection in 1920 proved to be a record, £394 5s 8d, and was pronounced as 'astonishing as times are bad'.

In 1929 expenditure for the anniversary service included the sum of 19s 9d as 'caps had to be provided for 21 small children who were singing'. These would be small girls. It was the custom of the time for female heads to be covered in church and these parents, probably because of poverty, had not supplied the necessary bonnets.

In 1933 the granddaughter of David Stott left the school a legacy of £100 and also returned the silver tea service which had been presented to him in 1833. The tea service was displayed for many years in a glass case in the secretary's room. After closure it became part of the Cathedral collection of silver.

Fund Raising

Although fund raising was always high on the agenda, the Committee rejected an offer of £30 per annum from the Manchester Bill Posting Company as 'it was not considered advisable to let the gable end for advertisements'; indeed the proposal that a board be erected to advertise the Sunday school itself was defeated in committee.

Room lets to outside organisations continued to be rigorously monitored. The school's own activities took precedence and lets such as those for orchestral rehearsals were not permitted on Fridays when they might disturb the Lit. Regular lets continued to include the Manchester and Northern Counties Ornithological Society, both for meetings and for their annual bird show, but when overtures were made in 1922 'to make the Bennett Street Schools their headquarters' the suggestion '[was] not entertained'. An application from the Manchester Talmud Torah School for the use of a room 'for the purpose of teaching Hebrew' was 'rejected with regret'. Organisations with diocesan, civic or charitable connections were considered more compatible: approaches from the Sunshine Guild and the National Union of Women Teachers were approved. The 12th Manchester Old Comrades Association applied to use the lecture hall for a Christmas party for 250 children. This was agreed. However when these same Old Comrades wished to hold a whist drive a few months later the committee voted against it. The rector applied for rooms for his church meetings and in 1929 'the Town Hall authorities... claimed the us[e] of the Lecture Hall for the purpose of taking the poll at the forthcoming general election'.

The subject of raffles was raised in 1929 but 'after a good deal of discussion' no decision was reached. The new rector was consulted in 1930 but 'would express no opinion'. The subject was again raised in 1932 under the chairmanship of another new rector, the previous incumbent having died in office, but he did not wish the church to be implicated in gambling. The Bishop had requested no raffles in Sunday schools but, again demonstrating its independence, Bennett Street explained the position 'from our point of view', and formally resolved that if raffles were being considered by individual societies, application should be made to the Committee of Management in the first instance.

Religion

The quality of the Sunday lessons was always under review. After 1918 the teachers' quarterly meetings were revived with the innovation that the older scholars also attended. A reorganised pattern of services included the commemoration of Armistice Day, following a nationally introduced format.

To help with music a sight-singing class for men only was started in 1925.

In 1922 the rector drew attention to training weekends for Sunday school teachers arranged by the Diocesan Sunday School Committee and also to the first annual gathering of Sunday school workers held at Manchester's Houldsworth Hall. The Diocesan Sunday School Manual was therefore purchased and lessons based upon it. On the initiative of the teachers themselves advice was sought from Stockport Sunday School to 'ascertain how the kindergarten system of teaching is applied'. Stockport Sunday School was non-denominational and of immense influence in the movement; it served a mostly mill community six miles south of Manchester.

Teachers' wayward time-keeping gave cause for comment although, as the committee was well aware, the rules were difficult to enforce because of the greater travelling distances now involved. Most unusually for Bennett Street, its supply of teachers in waiting seemed to have evaporated and in the 1930s an appeal for recruits to the teaching ranks was made in school, at social gatherings and also in the day school.

Education

By 1920 the Manchester Education Committee was anxious that the Grantham Scholarships should be re-instated following their war-time suspension, and during the interwar years candidates sat the examinations and subsequently took up their places at the Manchester College of Technology.

The Lit

The Literary and Educational Society was in its 76th year in 1919 and continued to meet weekly. Although the Lit had continued throughout the war numbers had decreased and by the 1930s there were 85 members. By 1934 they were increasingly aware of the travelling involved for those who worked in the city, returned home for tea and then travelled back to school for the Lit. This was thought to be a fruitless exercise and from this date onwards a tea was provided at school. The interwar syllabus included dramatic play readings, often of Shakespeare 'cleverly abridged'; music papers illustrated by excerpts played on the piano by one of the members and evenings devoted to holiday travel. Talks were given by one member who travelled widely on business, for example to India, Japan and Germany, and was able to report first-hand on his impressions of those countries. Such experiences were rare at that time and these contributions were always eagerly anticipated. Other evenings were devoted to the reading of members' original short stories and to impromptu speeches. The dramatic section gave its first postwar production in 1920. With the exception of the war years the Lit hosted a Christmas Conversazione, which was open to all school members and friends. They played cerebral games, sang glees and carols, had country dancing and partook of a supper. This was perhaps the only occasion at Bennett Street when coffee as well as tea was served.

Welfare and Charity

The school's autonomy from St Paul's church remained apparent in 1922 when the rector sought permission for a performance of the pantomime of *Rip van Winkle* to be given in aid of the church steeple. This was agreed but 'children in arms not admitted'. The school's own organisations gave occasional donations towards the school, for example the Girls' Friendly Society gave 10s 6d in 1921, and in the same year the adult class gave £100 towards a new boiler. The scouts gave the proceeds of their 1923 social to the Hospital Saturday Committee and each year throughout the period performances of the pantomime were presented in aid of Ancoats Hospital. When this hospital asked various churches in the area to help run a stall at its three day Bazaar in aid of a new x-ray department, Bennett Street minutes noted that at the inaugural meeting 'nobody turned up except our own people'.

Whit Week

The post-war revival of the Whit Monday procession took place in 1919. In 1924 it was decided that 'we ask a policeman to accompany us to the end of Oldham Street'. Was traffic becoming heavier on the Oldham Road and assistance required for a procession to turn right out of Bennett Street? The processional route on the return from Albert Square was via Cathedral Street, Cannon Street, High Street, Thomas Street, Oak Street and back to school. In 1926 the General Strike put the procession (and the outings) in jeopardy; only a week before they thought there would be no excursion trains but on the Saturday of the Whit Weekend the press reported a 'holiday rush to the sea' and two days later the Walk took place with sunshine and smiles, 20,000 children in the procession, and record crowds to support them.[5]

Bennett Street had always prided itself on its hospitality, in fact 'everyone welcome' could have been its motto. Following the amalgamation with the adjoining parishes, in 1929 children from other schools, principally St Michael and St Thomas were invited to join the Bennett Street procession and also to take part in the sports days.

St Michael's church offered a donation to cover the expenses incurred in providing the free buns and milk for their own children but this was politely declined and the hospitality confirmed in a note: 'we extend[ed] to them a welcome to all our festivities in Whit Week'.

After a hesitant start in 1919 the school re-established a full programme of Whit Week outings in 1920 and were encouraged to save up for them by paying into a new Whit Week Savings Club (the Penny Bank set up in 1851 having closed during the war). Under the new arrangements contributions of one penny upwards were taken each Sunday. No withdrawals were permitted until the annual pay out on a convenient date prior to Whit Sunday. The fact that this bank operated on a Sunday meant that it could be for school members only, otherwise the leaders would have classed it as 'trading' and this they would not have sanctioned on the Sabbath.

There were field sports on the Wednesday and Thursday and an adult full-day outing on the Friday. On that occasion they travelled by the 8.30 am train from London Road station (now Piccadilly) to Prestbury, from where they walked to Capesthorne for tea. They then walked on to Chelford, returning by the 8.37pm to Manchester. From the late 1920s and into the 1930s the Whit Friday destinations included York and Grange-over-Sands; and then in 1937 they became even more adventurous and, via Thomas Cook & Son, they travelled by rail to London. The cost of £1 6s 3d included two meals with a surcharge of one shilling per member 'for a saloon'. Similar arrangements were made in 1938 to travel to Edinburgh. These were substantial costs; at this time a textile weaver's weekly wage was about 36s 6d and the London trip cost 26s 3d, so perhaps it is not surprising that a less expensive arrangement was requested and Windermere was chosen.

Although the organisation of the Whit Week outings had continued, by 1936 the numbers taking part had dropped dramatically. A week's holiday with pay was now commonplace and many members were choosing to travel independently. Those attending the children's sports day dropped from 229 in 1920 to forty-nine in 1935; the adults participating in the Friday outing dropped from ninety-nine in 1920 to forty-seven in 1935.

From 1924 a cricket match was organised on Whit Saturday afternoon between the school's cricket team and the rest of the school. This proved a popular event which continued into the 1930s but it was not always without mishap. In 1932 the Committee of Management minutes noted a significant crockery breakage at the cricket field: '14 cups, 7 small plates, 5 saucers, 2 large plates, 1 basin, 1 milk jug'. No explanation is given but it is to be hoped that the breakages occurred after the tea interval!

Social Activities

The festive season parties of 1918/1919 were free to returning service men, a compassionate but fundamental change in policy. At the teachers' Christmas party held on 26 December 1919 one of the artistes was Madam Bella Baillie who in later life achieved world prominence as Dame Isobel Baillie. For Bennett Street she sang 'Deep in my heart a lute laid hid' and 'The bird I love the best' both by Florence Aylward and 'I think' by D'Hardelot. She also sang a duet with Mr Leech, 'The Voyagers' by Sanderson.

The tickets for the 1919 New Year's Eve party were '6d each plus [war]tax, after tea the same', and on New Year's Day there was a 'sweet tea (i.e. no savoury course) at 9d plus tax, after tea the same'; oranges were on the menu in 1923. These prices remained static throughout the interwar period, a reflection perhaps on the economic depression being experienced. The need to avoid waste was particularly noted in 1931 when two ladies were 'empowered to check the food coming into the school [for the parties]…and to supervise the cutting up'; a demanding task, in view of the parties' popularity and the fact that sliced bread was not yet available to them. The Christmas day free treat for the teachers was, 'after considerable discussion', abolished in September 1934, but before December this decision was revised; the party was held but by priced ticket.

Bennett Street teas were preceded by the singing of a grace. Led by the organ playing the Old Hundredth, to which more usually the words 'All people that on earth do dwell' were set, they sang:

> 'Be present at our table Lord, /Be here and everywhere adored, These creatures bless and grant that we /May feast in paradise with Thee'.

And at the end of the meal they sang:

> 'We thank Thee Lord for this our food, /But more because of Jesus' blood.
> Let manna to our souls be given, /The bread of life sent down from heaven'.

As the school did not boast a hot water supply, the used crockery was placed in large tin baths to await the 'washing-up party'.

After the First World War a pantomime became the standard New Year entertainment. In addition to the usual titles of *'Cinderella'* (1928) and *'Ali Baba'* (1931), there was *'Thud and Blunder'* in 1930 and *'The Enchanted Cat'* in 1932. At this period the pantomimes were written by one of the members, Mr Goode, who, even when he removed to London, continued to supply the scripts each year. In 1939 they departed from their norm and performed a non-stop revue.

Although the type of entertainment varied, the singing of the canticle by the audience always opened the proceedings.

It was during the interwar period that the Bennett Street social scene reached its zenith. In response to external criticism the leaders declared that not only did it help the Sunday school, but it aimed to 'educate our girls and boys to become real Christian men and women…we are doing the right work'. The societies flourished, the Lit being described as 'healthy', the social club as 'prosperous', the scouts 'progressive' and the women's class 'active'. New societies and sports clubs proliferated. The Committee of Management gave permission for the formation of the individual clubs but took no part in running them, nor did they subsidise them.

Within the first year of peace the various indoor clubs, such as the billiards and chess, merged into one overall social club. It had its own room and was further enhanced by a canteen which opened on two evenings a week; it was pronounced 'a boon not only for the young people but also for the greybeards of the staff'. Clubs which had been in abeyance during the war, for instance cricket, cycling and swimming, were re-started and a regular schedule of country rambles was introduced. A football club was formed in 1923; a ladies' hockey club in 1925, and a tennis club in 1926. A 'Shakesperian Club' is mentioned for the first time in the 1920s as is a historians' class. The cricket club won the league in 1931. The billiards team received congratulations in 1933 for 'winning the Shield and medals awarded by the leagues'. These clubs all held socials, concerts or whist drives; the men's class also held smoking concerts - live music for men only with smoking permitted.

During the 1930s the cricket club's winter entertainment became more sophisticated. From 1935 they held an annual 'soiree', a black tie occasion held in the lecture hall with a supper served in No. 2 room.[6]

The popularity of the parties and the pantomimes caused the purchase of additional chairs as volunteers were continually sought to transport chairs from the first floor tea room to the ground floor lecture hall. Similarly the pots committee, in charge of the crockery and cutlery, was galvanised into action 'there being only two dozen knives and three dozen forks in the school'.

This increased social activity also generated extra work for the caretaker. During term time the building was, with the activities of the day school, the Sunday school and the outside lets, in use twelve hours a day. During the period the lady caretaker (the widow of the previous incumbent) retired with a lump sum of £12 11s 0d and a new caretaking couple was appointed. This was a joint appointment with the MEC who issued an eighteen point schedule of the dusting, sweeping and cleaning duties required, for example cleaning of hearthstone, black leading of grates and 'fires to be made up at noon'. The Sunday school benefited from this, their additional requirements being re-arrangement of the furniture for evening events and Sunday services and ensuring Sunday heating. The premises were also to be 'kept clear of intruders'. The service charge for washing up at socials (for 140-180 the charge was 7s 6d; 180-220 10 shillings; over 220 12s 6d) was charged to the organisers of the respective socials.

In 1925 there is the first mention of non-school attenders being members of organisations such as the scouts and the sports clubs. It was 'generally understood that as long as [the individuals] conformed to the rules of the School, there was no objection'. The leaders found however that non-attenders brought outside influences and ideas and began to make efforts to modernise the school's traditional ways. In particular the ladies' hockey club challenged the finishing time of socials and the committee's long-held opinions regarding selling and collecting cash on school premises. In 1927 the hockey club applied to hold a social with a finishing time of 10.30 pm. The committee granted the let 'subject to [the normal] 10 pm close'. The request was repeated in 1928 and was again refused. However later that year the minutes record that 'after a long discussion' the committee voted in favour of a 10.30 pm close for all socials. The vote was by no means unanimous, eleven votes in favour and seven against. The committee took the opportunity afforded by the time concession to remind all clubs that socials were socials and not 'dances', even though they were now held on a polished dance floor, and that the rule 'four items other than dancing must be provided' would be strictly enforced.

The hockey club proposed the sale of sweets and ice cream at the Christmas and New Year parties although the committee insisted that there should be no pressure used in the selling and in 1934 they applied to run a Christmas club; again permission was granted with the proviso that they did not collect for it on a Sunday.

An innovation during the interwar period was the use of the lecture hall by individual school members for family occasions such as golden weddings, 21st birthday celebrations and wedding breakfasts. One male teacher, although he did not use the hall, was allowed to borrow 'one trestle table, four forms, three table cloths and two tea urns for his wedding'.

In March 1939 the scouts performed their show *'On Top of the World'*, but by then Bennett Street itself was not on top of the world and the morning service for older boys was discontinued because of decreased numbers.[7]

When war was declared in September 1939, the Committee of Management announced that all Bennett Street activities would be cancelled until further notice 'owing to the restrictions placed on the general public by the Government through the War with Germany', and fixed its next meeting for a Saturday afternoon so that it could be held in daylight.

WILLIAM ASHTON: DIED 1934

When William Ashton died Bennett Street acknowledged his untiring work in the school and his rare qualities of leadership. He had been a Bennett Street Sunday School teacher and a manager, a member of the Committee of Management, serving a term as its chairman, and he had become a trustee.

In his youth Ashton was one of the two young men (the other was Andrew Dean) who rescued two scholars who fell into deep water during a Bennett Street outing to Betws-y-Coed on Whit Friday 1893. They had 'at once jumped after them and brought them safely to land'. For this action they were awarded certificates from the Royal Humane Society, subsequently presented to them by the Lord Mayor of Manchester.

By profession Ashton was a local day school teacher and later a headmaster. He had a great interest in sport. In the Sunday school magazine he is described as:

> *'... renowned as one who could bowl out a team some Saturday afternoons, a hero as fullback for Blackley, he did perhaps more than any other one person for Children's sports [in the city], working madly for those early Belle Vue sports days, afterwards for the upbuilding of schoolboy football. We too benefited always from his love of, his interest in sport. Our cycling club people, then our cricketers [and our ladies'] hockey team... Right to the end he had been one to whom youth could come for*

inspiration and help. On field days of yore his high spirits drew into the fun everyone near: no one felt out of it with him around.

His lessons in the Select [Class], his favourite treatments of the Sermons of "Robertson of Brighton", moulded numerous young men in critical years. From the founding of the Grantham Scholarships his time has unsparingly been used in the interests of each and every candidate.... How many of us, saved from ourselves at times by his inexhaustible patience, are presenting something like a front to Life because of these scholarships and [now we have lost our] opportunity of being tender and patient towards him in turn!

'We have for long looked up to Mr Ashton as our chief man. He "kept the ring" in the Committee of Management and had a lively interest in Scouts and Girl Guides, in every section of the work in Church and Schools. His quizzical grimace or the pat on the head, has made many a little No.1 laddie feel he had a big friend.'

In 1934 William Ashton was mourned by a 'sorrowing wife and relatives'. His son, his only child, was killed during World War I, in 1915 at Gallipoli, aged 25. His first wife died in 1916.

It was William Ashton who unveiled the war memorial tablet in the school in 1921, and when he died in 1934 the school remembered him as 'so stalwart a champion, such an upright Christian gentleman'.[8]

William Ashton appears on the Committee of Management photograph of 1930 and that of the Whit Week Cricket Match in the same year.

9

[1843-1940]

The Bennett Street Day School

Historians record that 'earnest middle class promoters of Sunday schools often became involved, too, in the promotion of day schools'.[1] The Bennett Street Sunday School leaders are numbered amongst these earnest promoters, operating a day school on their premises from 1843 until 1939.

They saw their mission as the education of 'thousands' of children from the surrounding 'densely populated and neglected portion of our city…who might otherwise have grown up uncared for and uninstructed'. They possessed a large building specifically built to operate as a Sunday school with weekday evening classes. It was empty for a good portion of the week and therefore available for use as a day school.

Successive Factory Acts during the second half of the nineteenth century limited the time children could be in work and therefore increased the time available for their education. Originally Sunday schools had catered for the children of the destitute but by the mid-nineteenth century those attending were largely children of the 'deserving poor' defined as 'honest, industrious and in difficulties through no fault of their own'. Research revealed that the working class parents interested in educating their children, and prepared to pay for it, were not a 'distinct economic or occupational group' but one which cut across these definitions, a 'socio-religious' group intent on acquiring 'self respect and … respectability'.[2]

It was in 1843 that a Mrs Gibbons applied to the Bennett Street Sunday School Committee of Management for permission to use the lower boys' room to start an infant day school. This was agreed; it was to be called the Bennett Street Infants School. It was to be inspected by the Sunday school's Visitors and charged fees of 2d per week in advance, unlike the Sunday school where tuition was free.

The Sunday school had always had a good name in the area as a friendly and caring establishment and by the end of the first year parents had enrolled 139 of their children there. It is likely that many of these parents were, or had been, members of the Sunday school. As the day school grew both in numbers and in scope, soon incorporating infants, juniors and seniors, responsibility for it passed from Mrs Gibbons to St Paul's Schools' Committee.[3]

This *modus operandi* continued up to the 1870 Education Act, and beyond it until 1903 when responsibility for the day school was transferred from the Schools' Committee to the local authority. The expenses of the building, such as lighting, heating and water, were then shared between the Bennett Street trustees and the Manchester School Board, as was the successive purchase of more up-to-date furniture such as desks, and equipment such as pianos. The board seems to have borne the cost of decorating. This arrangement was of great benefit to the Sunday school and one which in later years became vital to its ability to continue.

This new situation also required the regularisation of various previously *ad hoc* understandings. For instance, from this date the day school would use only certain designated rooms and the caretaker's wage became a shared cost and a municipal job description was issued for him. The Sunday school continued to take responsibility for his coals and gas and also provided items such as 'a suitable top coat'.

Mrs Gibbons' initiative had proved immediately popular and by 1850 the number enrolled had risen to 300, and for the following 50 years hovered between 300 and 400; a reduction of about one hundred in the 1860s could perhaps be attributed to the onset of the Cotton Famine and parental inability to meet non-essential expenditure; also other day schools were opening in the area. A new church with a day and Sunday school opened on nearby Blossom Street in 1860 and further churches were built in the district in the 1870s[4]. The passing of the Education Act in 1870, which introduced for the first time compulsory state elementary education, resulted in an increase of approximately 65 per cent over the 1860 figure.

Similar standards to those of the Sunday school were required of the day scholars: 'Strict attention will be paid to enforce habits of obedience, punctuality and cleanliness and such things as tend to form the moral character of the children'. The ban on selling in the Sunday school extended to the day school also; in 1929 matches and almanacks had been sold in aid of their own sports fund but after intervention by the Committee of Management the headmaster 'could promise that the offence would not be repeated'.

Whilst under the jurisdiction of the Schools' Committee the day school had continued to be inspected by the Sunday school Visitors but in 1864, pre-dating Forster's Education Act of 1870 by six years, the Bennett Street day school had been externally inspected for the first time and was under the control of certificated teachers; by the 1880s there is evidence that it was receiving a government grant.

From the day school's inception Mrs Gibbons charged fees, called 'school pence'. From the 1850s to the 1870s these were between 2d and

4d per week (infants were free) the poor paying a penny. The very few (not more than ten) found to be too poor to pay received financial assistance from the funds of the Bennett Street Sunday School committee. From 1895 onwards juniors were free also, the seniors by then paying one penny per week.

The day school was divided into juniors (Standards I and II) and seniors (Standards III to VI) with separate classes for boys and girls. In the early years of the school the children over the age of nine were likely to have been part-timers, spending half their day in work and half at school. In 1893 all classes were mixed and by 1908 a Standard VII class had been added. The headmaster had a staff of six teachers, with a separate head for the infants assisted by two further teachers. School hours were 9 am until 12 noon and 2pm until 4.30pm.

Being a church school, scholars attended service at St Paul's each Ash Wednesday and Ascension Day as a body and all were taught scripture history. The juniors were taught reading, spelling, writing, arithmetic, geography, English grammar, music (tonic sol-fa), girls' sewing, drawing and elementary science. The curriculum for the senior department included the junior subjects with the additions of history and geometry. The older girls were taught sewing and cutting out while the boys had lessons in advanced drawing and 'manual work'. Progress was 'tested quarterly by private [examination] and annually by public examination, and prizes awarded'.

The infants department had mixed classes and learned reading, spelling, writing, arithmetic, sewing, kindergarten drawing and outlines of natural history; an annual report noted that they were 'taught and managed with kindness and very general success'.

After 1903 the building was subject to inspection by both the government inspectors (HMIs) and by the board. Through the years the Bennett Street trustees adapted the building to comply with government requirements and later with those of the Manchester School Board, for instance by erecting moveable partitions in the large rooms to create separate classrooms. Between the wars the state of the flooring caused concern and the board suggested that the upper floors should not be used for 'dancing or drilling of a strenuous nature'. At this inner city school, which possessed only a very small playground referred to as 'the yard', outside games and sports are not mentioned, but scholars were said to do well in their swimming.

The 1920 HMI inspection revealed that the playground was considered 'quite inadequate'; the stairs were found to be no longer flat but unevenly hollowed by a hundred years of clattering boots and were declared narrow and dangerous; additional partitions were required for the two rooms which housed several classes.

Bennett Street records show that in 1925 the Manchester authorities considered the building to be unsuitable as a modern day school and in 1926 it was put on their 'Black List'. In spite of this decision the school's annual report recorded 1926 as being 'quite a normal year'. With 351 scholars the Schools' Committee considered it was still making a significant contribution to elementary education in the neighbourhood, although in 1929 it was realistic enough to note that they did not think it would be passed as an upper school.

Of course the minutes record only the days which stand out from the common round. In 1930 there was the notable day when all the children were declared free from infectious disease; in 1933 one of the inspectors recommended the purchase of new Bibles and prayer books (for which the board would pay) and there was the excitement of the acquisition of a dolls' house by the infant department; in 1934 there is a reference to 'lunch being served in the school'. External activities included a party of scholars travelling to London to visit the Wembley Exhibition in 1924 and six scholars having pictures accepted for a city-wide collection of scholars' work exhibited at the Manchester City Art Gallery in 1933. On at least two occasions in the early twentieth century the day school staged an open day so that parents could visit, and in 1933 a class, advised by a lady from the board, was held for mothers to discuss the dressing and clothing of children.

But there were disappointments too. The proposal to form an old scholars association was turned down as was the headmaster's request in 1930 to have a wireless set installed for teaching purposes. Broadcasting had started only in 1927 and although the board was said to welcome this progressive move, they would not fund it, nor would the Bennett Street committee sanction a collection for it in the Sunday school. The matter was therefore left in abeyance and no further mention was made of it in the records.

From 1934 much of the small domestic property surrounding the school was demolished and was replaced by industrial units of varying types; this scheme sounded the death knell of the Bennett Street day school. By 1936 the number of scholars had dropped to 188 and three of the teachers had been redeployed. Following the 1935 inspection the board finally condemned the playground and by 1939 it was obvious that structural alterations to the school had become essential. It proved impossible to implement these and with only 87 scholars now on the books the managers gave notice that the school would close within eighteen months, at Easter 1940.

However the declaration of the Second World War intervened and the school closed abruptly in October 1939, the children being evacuated to Marten near Blackpool. This evacuation did not last long. The school reopened very briefly in January 1940 when approximately fifty percent of the children had already returned home, but the board considered the danger caused by the close proximity to the railway goods yard was too great and decided to use alternative premises.

Bennett Street Day School closed finally on 31 March 1940.

10

1939-1945

The Second World War

In the months preceding the start of the Second World War in September 1939 it became apparent that England was about to experience the reality of modern warfare for the first time, through enemy bombing of the big cities. The government was also concerned with the Spanish Civil War and, of course, the perennial problems associated with social reform; education and poverty remained. On the declaration of war places of entertainment closed and the assembly of crowds was forbidden. Men were once again conscripted, as were women without family responsibilities; women also did war work, for example in munitions factories and, as in World War I, took over the jobs of the absent males. A nation-wide black-out was enforced with interior lighting restricted and outside lights banned; Bank Holidays were cancelled and food rationing introduced.

In Manchester the Trafford Park industrial estate was heavily involved in the production of armaments and other war-time engineering work, thus rendering the area, along with the adjacent port of Manchester, a prime target for enemy bombers. In December 1940 a large portion of the city centre's business area was destroyed in the Manchester Blitz. The Hallé Orchestra lost its home, the Free Trade Hall, in this action but the appointment of John Barbirolli as conductor in 1943 marked the beginning of a resurgence in the Manchester music scene.[1]

Immediately on the outbreak of war Bennett Street, following government regulations, cancelled all social activities 'with one exception' but quite quickly afterwards, in October 1939, the Committee of Management minuted their decision that 'any society desirous of [re]starting its activities shall apply for permission' to that committee. By 1940 the school had settled once again into a war-time routine.

The Building

Bennett Street Sunday School, as a large building near to the city centre, was conveniently placed to play its part in the war effort. The Air Raid Welfare Office used it as part of their rest centre service; the lecture hall was rented out to Manchester Corporation Education Committee and to the ARP (Air Raid Precautions) Shelter Department for storage of their bunks. These lets provided welcome revenue. During the blitz the fire brigade used the roof as a vantage point from which to fight the blaze raging in the LMS (London Midland and Scottish) railway goods yard on the opposite side of Thompson Street. The school building remained intact, as did the church. The second night of the blitz targeted the Piccadilly area.[2]

Administration

Immediately prior to World War I in 1914 the topic of scholar numbers had been the leaders' primary concern but in 1939, although numbers had continued to reduce relentlessly during the inter-war years, it was their day school which was exercising the minds of the Bennett Street committees. The closure of the day school in 1940 resulted in a situation which had a profound effect on the running of the Sunday school, as its presence had meant that the Manchester Education Authority had shared the expenses involved in the upkeep of the building. When it closed all expenses became the sole responsibility of the Sunday school. The burden was considerable and quickly became literally unbearable. With the closure of the day school the Schools' Committee no longer had a purpose. It was disbanded in 1946.

The Committee of Management met on Saturday afternoons rather than on the usual week-day evening and consulted the Corporation Surveyor regarding the most suitable assembly point should evacuation of the building be necessary during school hours.

Anniversary Sunday

During the war it was found impossible to retain the usual format for the anniversary services. With the church's evening service re-scheduled to the afternoon it was agreed that for the duration of the war the anniversary services would be held on one December Sunday and the collection taken in the school on the following Sunday afternoon. This single collection was still producing around £200 and remained the primary source of income. Letters were written to subscribers explaining that activities were necessarily curtailed but it was hoped that the school's religious and social work would continue when the war was over. The subscribers remained loyal; all the usual subscriptions were received and many were accompanied by encouraging letters.

Religion

This was the background against which the school operated in 1939 for the law against assembly did not apply to places of worship; it was a situation of fewer men, less income, less heating, reduced lighting within and dark streets outside. A war-time schedule was drawn up and the Sunday afternoon services continued, albeit with reduced numbers (in 1940 average attendance was 58, and by 1942 this had dropped to 43). In the early days of the war all scholars combined for service in No 2 room but later just the younger ones had joint services. These services started earlier, at 2 pm, to ensure that the children arrived home before dark. The church re-timed its evening service to Sunday afternoon. The annual armistice commemoration service was discontinued.

Just one example of the difficulties encountered in operating in war time was the fact that towards the end of the war five girls moved up from the lower room to the upper, but 'there was no hope of the older boys of No 1 being transferred to No 2 until such time as a teacher could be found'. The majority of male teachers at that point remained away on war service.

Prizes

Teachers' prizes were discontinued and were never re-instated, whilst scholars' prizes were retained, but only for the young ones.

The Lit

The Literary and Educational Society was the one society which continued to meet without interruption. At the start of the war when all the other societies ceased their activities, the Lit committee justified their decision to continue by considering themselves an educational society rather than a social one, but the fact that they were due to celebrate their centenary in 1943 may have had some bearing on it. They considered it would be 'deplorable if we could not continue'. The Lit did continue but in a modified form, moving into a small room to conserve light and heat, starting at 6.30pm, finishing at 8pm and giving only one paper per evening.

In 1941, in The Lit's 99th year, they met only in September and October, March and April to avoid the darkest months and arranged their summer excursions to locations near to the homes of members so that tea could be taken in their gardens.

At the start of their centenary session war-time restrictions had become too severe to allow the organisation of an appropriate celebration but the centenary syllabus included two evenings devoted to reminiscences about the society, the school and the area. In his opening address the president, J H Hobbins, remarked that although the character of the general meeting 100 years ago seemed to have been much the same as it was in the 100th session, he considered that the society, originally established at Bennett Street for the self-education of the working class, had retained an innate vitality and it was that which had ensured its survival.

Odds and Ends Magazine

The Lit's Manuscript Magazine, *'Odds and Ends'* continued to be produced throughout the war. It was stated that 'we are living in extraordinary times and short articles [about war-time conditions] written from the personal angle would be valuable in years to come'. One of these articles records one member's experiences on the morning after the 1940 Manchester Blitz. It describes their bus journey to get to work on the morning of Monday 23 December 1940; travelling down Rochdale Road from North Manchester they had discovered that 'the LMS [railway] Goods Station at Thompson Street was ablaze' and how one of the fire fighters had allayed their anxiety by reporting that the school and the church were still standing.[2]

Whit Week

In 1940 Manchester's Central Committee for the Whit Monday processions sought church opinion regarding war-time arrangements, again in the light of government restrictions on assembly. Alternative suggestions were tabled: that each church process round its own parish; that processions be held at different times in different districts; that Whit Monday observance be abandoned altogether. Bennett Street favoured the latter option and there is no further reference in the minutes to processions or to associated Whit Week festivities until 1944 when the younger children were taken to Belle Vue circus. In March 1945 the Central Committee suggested a procession; Bennett Street remained of the opinion that it should not be considered until after the war. However, for whatever reason, by April that decision had been reversed and they had resolved to participate.

Charity

Charitable efforts were continued. After the initial ban in 1939, the nation's social activities had been re-established quite quickly and in 1940 certain Bennett Street organisations such as the scouts were meeting again and general whist drives and jumble sales were being held in aid of school and church funds. The school continued to support the Ancoats Hospital by giving the proceeds of a concert and in addition, as Whit Week was not being 'kept up', they also donated the interest from the Whit Week fund. The 'St Paul's Church and Bennett Street Sunday School National Savings Group' was formed in June 1940.

Social Activities

A reduced social scene, but certainly including whist drives, was once more operating by 1940 and a comforts fund was again organised with parcels and Christmas cards being sent to the scholars and teachers serving with the forces. A duplicator was purchased for £2 so that the scouts' magazine could be circulated to troop members away on war service. The 1939 minutes indicate that the discussion of parties for the festive season was 'left over' and no further reference to this subject is found until after the war.

———————— * ————————

There is a lack of information about those on active service in World War II. Details of fatalities for the First World War were recorded in the annual reports of the time, but the printing of these reports ceased in 1940. Although after the Second World War a

'Grand Reunion of Bennett Streeters, particularly those returning from the forces, war work, etc.' was held and was pronounced 'such a success', no details of numbers serving in the war have been found and the sole indication of fatalities is that in March 1956 a new position for the war memorial was considered and the names from the 1939-45 war were to be recorded on it.

And what of the future? As early as July 1942 the trustees thought it advisable to discuss the post-war future of the school but the matter was deferred; in 1944 the lady teachers from No 4 room asked the Committee of Management whether anything was being done regarding post-war plans. The answer had been negative 'the end of the war being too far off'. It was not until May 1945 that a sub-committee was appointed to consider the post-war operation of the school.

11

1945-1966

Post War Decline

The post-war period was one of austerity and shortages, seemingly of everything: food, clothes, coal, housing, and also of skilled tradesmen. Working hours had been reduced compared with those of pre-war years; prices rose dramatically. Nuclear war was an ever-present threat. The country was finally freed from war-time food rationing in 1954; the Clean Air Act was passed in 1956. Air travel and holidays abroad became increasingly affordable and popular, and those who had learned to drive as part of the war effort were beginning to acquire cars and were using them for family outings on a Sunday afternoon, an activity completely at variance with the culture of the Sunday School Movement. This was the post-war situation with which all Sunday schools struggled.

King George VI died in 1952 and was succeeded by his daughter Queen Elizabeth II.

The Manchester planners were faced with the rebuilding of the commercial centre of the city following the Blitz of 1940 and also had to contend with the problems associated with their slum clearance programme under which the housing in the school's immediate neighbourhood was scheduled for demolition. The corporation also embarked upon a policy of rationalisation of street names and in 1954 the Bennett Street in New Cross was changed to Bendix Street.

Bennett Street's chief anxiety was one of finance. Following the closure of the day school in 1940 the Manchester Education Committee no longer shared the costs of the building and equipment. The significance of this situation cannot be over-emphasised.

With the disbanding of the St Paul's Schools' Committee, all responsibility for the running of the Sunday school rested with the Committee of Management, with the trustees retaining responsibility for the building and the investments. During the war the number of trustees had been reduced to seven due to death, ill health and removal from the Manchester area and new trustees were appointed.

The Building

Shortly after the war an application was received from the Ministry of Works wishing to take over the building for use by the government. The trustees gave the swift response that 'the property is not for disposal nor are we prepared to let them rooms'. A further twenty years were to elapse before disposal did take place. But not all approaches were turned down. 'The threat of nuclear war was taken seriously enough for the government to review its civil defence programme' and in 1954 Manchester's Welfare Department asked if the building could be used as a rest centre 'in the event of war'. The trustees immediately agreed to this request, but fortunately this particular change of role was never required.[1]

The Bennett Street branch of the war-time National Savings Scheme was not disbanded until 1950 with the records stating that 'approx £10,000 has been invested through the Group since its inception'.

The winter of 1947 was extremely harsh and the school's plans for its resurgence suffered a setback. Numbers attending dropped dramatically; heating was unsure for coal was short everywhere and travelling the increased distances to school was difficult due to the severe weather conditions.

Immediately after the war the school was running with an annual deficit of between £70 and £90. The religious and social work was said to be progressing but due to the higher prices prevailing and the reduced membership most social events, rather than being self-supporting, were running at a loss. Retrenchment became the order of the day. Wastage was frowned upon; for a room booked until 10.30pm the instruction was issued that the lights were to be turned out at that time 'promptly – and not leave it until a little later'. Services such as clock maintenance and piano tuning, slid quietly into oblivion. Expenditure on the lecture hall was however authorised in order to comply with new legislation for public performances; extra fire extinguishers were installed and new folding chairs which could be joined together were purchased. It was also thought important that external window cleaning should continue so that the school appeared to be fully occupied, for with the demise of the day school the building was open only on Sundays and on weekday evenings. Modernising suggestions, for instance the installation of hot water and a telephone were mooted but with funds being scarce neither suggestion was ever implemented.

The war-time years of unavoidable neglect had taken their toll and the minutes tell a story of expenditure simply on repairs, plumbing and maintenance which seemed to be absolutely essential. The top floor of the building was deemed to be unsafe and henceforth was considered as part of the rafters. The early 1960s brought problems with the ancient coal-fired boiler, the ensuing discussion noting that the area was likely to become a smokeless zone. Heating remained a major and pressing concern partly because the system heated the whole school even if by this point only a few rooms were in use; in 1962 it was resolved to change to an oil fired boiler.

However all was not gloom during this period of struggle and final decline. There were welcome reminders of previous palmy days and of the strong loyalty felt to the school.

In 1952 the school received from Australia the gift of an embroidered tapestry depicting the exterior of 'St Paul's Bennett Street Sunday School erected by voluntary subscription in 1818'. This had been stitched in 1846 by Alice Alcock, (photograph on page 99) the donor's grandmother when she attended the school.

The Anniversary

The anniversary collection continued to amass around £300 despite the post-war reductions in attendance and the changes in circumstances. Following an advertisement in the Manchester press in 1954 it realised £318 and in 1959 when a supreme effort was requested, the sum raised was £325. After this date £300 was never reached again. A large-scale spring fair was organised in 1955 with L S Lowry present; it netted just over £158. The school societies with funds of their own, for example the Sick and Funeral Society, whose work was no longer so relevant following the founding of the welfare state, donated to the general school fund and the church council helped with Whit Week expenses. Whist drives and socials were now held in aid of school funds, as was the annual reproduction of the pantomime.

Fund Raising

The letting of rooms continued, for instance to the Boy Scout Movement, the Ornithological Society and the Bach Choir but, although it would have been lucrative, outside requests for rooms on Sunday evenings were resisted; this 'could not be considered' it being against the principles of the school.

Religion

In 1949 a special service was held in recognition of the 400th anniversary of the Book of Common Prayer and twelve men and five women became eligible to receive Diocesan Medals for either twenty-five or fifty years of service as teachers or managers.

While the trustees were preoccupied in preserving the building, the Committee of Management, following consultation with the various rooms, embarked upon a major reorganisation of the Sunday worship. The original identification of the single sex rooms by number was dropped and scholars were divided into mixed sex departments of primary (up to eight years old), junior (aged between eight and fourteen) and seniors in two groups (fourteen to eighteen and from eighteen to the age of thirty). All opened and closed their services together but had separate lessons. The young boys who had been unable to move up because their male teachers were in the forces, were at last able to do so and, as in 1918, the male scholars returning from the war were invited to join the men's class. At this time young men aged eighteen were drafted into the forces for two years of national service. Regular contact with the Bennett Street conscripts was maintained via the Benevolent Society.

Bennett Street had always boasted a numerically strong adult section, with the ladies by this point occupying No 3 room on the second floor. As there was no upper age limit to Sunday school attendance both men and women attended until they achieved their biblical three score years and ten, and beyond. Perhaps it is an indication that people were living longer when, after the war, it became apparent that the older ladies were beginning to find the two long flights of stairs to be two flights too many and arrangements were made for all the adults to use the lecture hall on the ground floor for Sunday worship. During the 1950s the Sunday services continued from these new found homes; the occasional hymn singing services were reinstated and were said to attract good attendances.

Because of resignations, chiefly due to removal from the area, the Bennett Street supply of teachers, always previously found to be in excess of requirements, finally deserted them, with particular difficulty being experienced in the senior section.

Prizes

The Bennett Street book culture survived both the war and the paper shortages; the library re-opened (until 1959) and scholars' prizes were re-introduced. The prizes which had been endowed in the earlier years of plenty, for example for proficiency in scriptural knowledge, were awarded once again but the eligibility was widened to scholars of either sex. In 1953 the primary, junior and senior scholars were each presented with a Book of Common Prayer in commemoration of the Coronation of Queen Elizabeth II.

The Lit

The Literary and Educational Society continued to meet. Post-war adaptations to their syllabus included the introduction of a Brains Trust on the lines of a popular radio programme of the time when a panel dealt with questions followed by discussion. During that same session one member gave a paper which he said resulted from a question asked by one of the boys he taught: what was the Judgement Hall like when Jesus was brought before Pilate? The speaker confessed that it was this query that had led him into a deep study of Roman history and archaeology. The dramatic section re-formed in 1946 with a presentation of *When we are Married* by J B Priestley; they continued to perform until the 1960s.

In 1947 attendance at meetings of the Lit was greatly reduced due to the severe winter but 1948 brought renewed enthusiasm and the innovation of a holiday film, a 'home movie', of the Lake District; subsequent criticism declared 'this kind of thing is new to the society and was in the nature of an experiment'. The experiment was in fact repeated the following year when a film of Ayrshire, the Burns country and the Highlands was pronounced a very fine show. That was the year too when, in a debate on crime, they concluded that it 'MUST not pay'. The 1950 syllabus included a guest speaker, Mrs Coppock, who had that year attended the Passion Play at Oberammergau in Bavaria, Germany; she returned the following year to speak on 'a comparison of Religious Literature in Mediaeval Times and Today'. There were also talks on Everest and Lloyds of London.

About this time the first written indication appears that the Lit's committee was conscious that they were not attracting younger members and that consequently their membership was reducing to a point where the viability of the society was questioned. Although they remained unanimous that they continue, from 1958 to 1960 the society met fortnightly, and from 1960 monthly. The president opened the 120th session in September 1962 by stating that the society had encouraged him to think for himself, had always sought the highest standards and had been a joy and inspiration to him. But the society was obviously struggling and the minute book ends in October 1962.

Charity

In spite of the parlous state of the finances the school's charitable customs remained ingrained and in the year before it was absorbed into the National Health Service a small donation was sent to Ancoats Hospital which had previously, in the school's more affluent times, received the proceeds of a performance of the pantomime. On the death of the King in 1952, a donation of five guineas was sent to the King George Memorial Fund.

Whit Week

The Whit Week savings club was still in operation and the school once more joined Manchester's Whit Monday Anglican procession when it re-started in 1945. However they never revived the tradition of providing their children with a free bun, inner city poverty in post-war austerity England apparently being considered in a different light from that of the nineteenth century. By 1954 there were insufficient older girls available to hold the cords of the one banner. Although the size of the Bennett Street contingent in the procession was variously described as 'reduced' or even 'small' the school did continue to take part until 1964.

The Whit Week outings recommenced modestly in 1946, but the following year the day-long trips were reintroduced with a visit to Llangollen. From the 1950s onwards there were intermittent cancellations due to lack of interest; only twenty-three people signed up in 1960. Personal car ownership amongst the more affluent school members was increasing and there was more opportunity to travel individually. The Saturday event took the form of a social, with a band, and a whist drive for those who did not wish to dance.

Social Activities

All parties were suspended during the war. However the New Year's Day party was reinstated in 1946 when gifts of food towards the tea were gratefully acknowledged. The first post-war party, on 1 January 1946, was a tea and a concert; in 1947 the pantomime was re-introduced. But the mid-1950s brought the first indication of there being insufficient adults available to mount such productions and by the early 1960s the evening's entertainment had reverted to a social of dancing, games and solos. There was no New Year's Day party in 1964. With the occasional variation of a visit to the circus at Belle Vue, the children's Christmas party with Father Christmas in attendance, continued until at least 1963 and their outings until 1964.

In order to re-establish the school's social culture, so strong during the interwar period and in abeyance during the war (with the exception of The Lit) all members were encouraged to join, or to re-join, at least one of the school's societies and to attend on at least one evening per week. Following its war work as a storage area (when the whole of the lecture hall had been packed from floor to ceiling with pallets housing goods of many kinds), the floor of the lecture hall was once again made suitable for dancing, the dramatic society offered three productions per annum and a regular weekly programme of socials and whist drives was organised; all these continued into the 1960s. The women's class re-convened and bought its own stove for cookery demonstrations; the youth club merged with the social club and re-opened for two evenings per week with games, handicrafts, play readings and discussion groups. Societies were granted extensions to their closing times, to 10.45pm and in the later 1950s even to 11pm. The guides and cubs re-started and the 2/9th Manchester scout troop achieved a den of their own on the premises which they could use at any time the building was open; with financial help from the Committee of Management they issued a newssheet named 'Woodsmoke'. After the Second World War the troop boasted a higher than average number of Queen's Scouts for the area. It also produced three County Commissioners for Greater Manchester.[2]

Among the events that did not survive the war were the evening classes, the teachers' Christmas tea and prizes, the New Year's Eve party, the parents' party, and Founder's Day. The demise of Founder's Day precluded the opportunity to present eulogies on the more recent worthies. One who would certainly have been included was:

ROWLEY D FLETCHER (1905–1980)

Having attended as a scholar from his early days, Rowley Fletcher rose from the ranks and served Bennett Street Sunday School for the rest of his life. He was successively appointed a teacher and a manager; he took part in all activities, served on sub-committees and in 1936 was nominated as a member of the Committee of Management; he subsequently became its secretary. He was appointed secretary to the trustees in 1949.

A widower since 1944, his time was devoted to his two daughters, his business activities as director of the cotton firm which he had entered as office boy, to his voluntary work with the scout movement and with Bennett Street. As secretary to both the Committee of Management and to the trustees he was charged with the administration of all Bennett Street business; the running of the school activities, the maintenance of the building, the overseeing of the investments and the school's contacts with external bodies. He became the lynch pin of the school and in its final days oversaw its closure and organised the establishment of the Bennett Street Educational Charity.

Over the years, many researchers and students working on Manchester's social history appealed to Rowley Fletcher for assistance. Such appeals were never turned away and his help continued to be available long after the school's closure and indeed up to his death. He was a fount of knowledge on all things Bennett Street.

Just one of those who sought his advice and knowledge was Shelley Rohde, L S Lowry's biographer. It was Rowley Fletcher who explained something of the ethos of Bennett Street to her; how one always 'went down' to Bennett Street and that

> *'"once one had become caught up in it, one went two or three times a week... There was always something going on: chess, the drama society, music, rambles, lectures. Most of one's friends were BSSS people". Often one's wife or husband turned out to be a BSSS person too'.[3]*

It could be added that Bennett Street friendships tended to last a lifetime and Rowley Fletcher was a generous and firm friend to many.

It was after a conversation with him that Shelley Rohde concluded that Bennett Street became 'almost a way of life'. That was true in the case of Rowley Fletcher as it was for many others, and Rowley Fletcher gave back more than most.[4]

Rowley Fletcher is pictured at the presentation of the tapestry of the school in 1952 on page 99.

12

1966

The Closure

The mid-1950s witnessed the first internal signs that the reduced membership was insufficient to run the school's activities. The Committee of Management experienced difficulties in appointing representatives to the various sub-committees which were therefore forced to operate with *ad hoc* volunteers and, as has already been mentioned, manning problems were experienced regarding the Whit Monday procession and the pantomime. Even so an external rumour that Bennett Street was to close was said to be 'without foundation' in 1960.

In 1957 the caretaker, Mr Joe Hammersley retired after thirty years of service and a couple of years later the rector, Rev L E Gowing, after a similarly lengthy period at St Paul's moved to a rural living. It therefore fell to the new rector, Rev George Henshaw, to preside over the closing days of Bennett Street Sunday School.

In a period which saw the closing of many inner-city Sunday schools, everything pointed to the fact that Bennett Street too was inexorably approaching the end of its life. No member of the Committee of Management however was prepared to propose a definite resolution regarding closure but an open meeting decided that no steps should be taken until after the bicentenary of St Paul's church in July 1965. Finally, at a well attended meeting of the Committee of Management the following resolution was passed in September 1966:-

> 'Because of the lack of numbers attending the school, because redevelopment plans make it improbable that there will be any influx of children into the area in the foreseeable future and since suitable arrangements can be made for the small number of scholars now attending Bennett Street to join other Sunday Schools, this Committee considers that the necessity for keeping Bennett Street Sunday School open no longer exists and recommends that no further services be held on Sunday afternoons after the close of service on Sunday October 30th 1966....'[1]

On 25 October 1966 the following letter appeared in the *Manchester Evening News* beneath the familiar etching of the school's façade:

'When 1,500 went to Sunday school

Many readers who have lived in the New Cross district of Manchester will know this building.

It is Bennett Street Sunday and Day School, built in 1818 to serve the working population and their families as an education and recreative centre. In the heyday of Sunday schools, some 1,500 scholars attended each Sunday seeking religious instruction. Now with the movement of population to the outer districts and the present application of Manchester Corporation compulsorily to purchase land and houses in the area the trustees consider the purposes for which the building was put up no longer exist. With great reluctance they have decided to discontinue the Sunday afternoon services.

The final service will be held in the school on Sunday, October 30, at 2.30 pm, followed by a thanksgiving service in St Paul's Church, New Cross at 3.30 pm.

Past members, associates of the school and their friends are invited to attend one or both of the services.

R D Fletcher,
Secretary to the Trustees'[2]

These final gatherings in both school and church were well attended and included a good number of old scholars and teachers, many of whom had travelled considerable distances. At the service in school, with Miss Dorothy Bamford in the chair, a lesson from St Luke was read by Mrs H Chadwick and an address was given by Mr J E Bancroft. Having been connected with Bennett Street for seventy years, he vividly recalled how the teaching of the gospel was always paramount; how educational opportunities were readily available and how the various parties and entertainments had helped to keep the members together, sealing many, life-long friendships. The memory of David Stott who founded the school in 1801, and that of Benjamin Braidley, were reverently recalled and the assembled members were informed that a great grand-daughter of David Stott was present at that final service. Mr Rowley Fletcher presented the last prizes for regular attendance to the remaining young scholars and Mr W M Nesbitt led the closing prayers which were followed by the singing of the Nunc Dimittis. Mr Arnold White was the organist for the service.

The thanksgiving service in church which followed took the form of an anniversary Sunday evensong with the school banner displayed and the choir being augmented by many old members; there was a 'fairly large' congregation. The service opened with the anthem 'Lift up your heads ye lofty gates'. The first lesson was read by Miss Mary Bamford from the Apocrypha, 'Let us now praise famous men' and the second lesson by Mr J E Bancroft from the last chapter of St Luke's gospel, 'The resurrection and the appearance of Jesus to his disciples'. The rector, Rev George Henshaw preached, initially explaining that he had been specifically asked to give the final address because of the emotional strain involved had a member of the school delivered it. He remarked that his own impression of Bennett Street was that throughout its long history it had been a power-house, producing giants of influence who had helped form the characters of each succeeding generation. He suggested that the gospel spread by those past giants of Bennett Street Sunday School had been scattered far and wide and could never be lost. The service concluded with the singing of Jackson's Te Deum. Mr George Thorp, the church organist and a life-long Bennett Street member presided at the organ.[3]

Afterword

The contents of the school were sold. A sum of money was given to Bowdon parish church for the upkeep of David Stott's grave, and to the diocese for a suitable memorial of the school. The remainder formed the Bennett Street Educational Foundation and it is through this Foundation (subsequently named the Bennett Street Charity) that the name of Bennett Street Sunday School lives on in the twenty-first century.

The caretaker's house was compulsorily purchased in 1966 under the slum clearance scheme, but the trustees noted that there was a 'lack of action' in demolishing the school; it suffered heavily at the hands of vandals prior to its eventual demolition in 1971. It was a sad end for a building which had been, in the words of the new rector, the base for the 'religious social and cultural benefits which the school had been instrumental in bringing to so many people during its 160 years of existence'.

The Bennett Street Charity

'BENNETT STREET CHARITY: The Bennett Street Educational Charity exists to promote the religious education of beneficiaries in accordance with the doctrines and principles of the Church of England, and awards exhibitions, scholarships, etc. tenable at any school, university or college approved by the trustees. It provides financial assistance for clothing, tools, instruments, etc. on entering a profession, trade or calling; for travel in pursuance of educational objects; and for the study of music or other arts. The trust also provides financial assistance to any charitable organisation in the City of Manchester for the advancement of education and the development of physical, mental and moral capacities through leisure-time activities.

Beneficiaries must be under 25 years of age, and in need of financial assistance. They, or their parents, must be resident in the City of Manchester.

The Trustees meet to consider applications in February, July and October. To be considered applications should be made by the 15th of the previous month to the Bennett Street Trustees, c/o Mr A Roberts, 54 Crumpsall Lane, Crumpsall, Manchester M8 6SG'.[4]

Sources and Footnotes

Chapter 1: Introduction: The Sunday School Movement

Sources:
- The archive of St Paul's Bennett Street Sunday School was lodged in Manchester Central Library, Local Studies Department: ref M/103.

Footnotes:
1. Authors including Thomas Walter Laqueur, *Religion and Respectability: Sunday Schools and Working Class Culture, 1780-1850*, (London, Yale University Press, 1976); K D M Snell, *The Sunday School Movement in England and Wales: Child Labour, Denominational Control and Working Class Culture'*, Past and Present No 164, August, 1999; A P Wadsworth, 'The First Manchester Sunday Schools', *Bulletin of the John Rylands Library, Vol. 33, No 2*, (March 1951); W R Ward, *Religion and Society in England 1790-1850*, (London, B T Batsford Ltd, 1972).
2. W R Ward, *Religion and Society*, p. 140.
3. John K Walton, *Lancashire, A Social History 1558-1939*, (Manchester, Manchester University Press, 1994) p. 104.
4. Ernest H Hayes, *Raikes, the Pioneer*, (London, The National Sunday School Union, 1930), pp. 15, 24.
5. Manchester Sunday School minutes 1784, Chetham's Library, Manchester, ref: A6.3; A Report on the present state of Sunday schools in Manchester,1788, Bennett Street archive ref: M/103/19/10.
6. T W Laqueur, *Religion and Respectability: Sunday Schools and Working Class Culture, 1780-1850*, (London, Yale University Press, 1976), p.64.
7. *Bennett Street Memorials* ,1904, Appendix p.28.
8. S J Davies, *'Classes and Police in Manchester 1829-1880*, in Kidd and Roberts (ed), *City Class and Culture: Studies of*

Social Policy and Cultural Production in Victorian Manchester, (Manchester, Manchester University Press, 1985), p. 32; F M L Thompson, *The Rise of Respectable Society: A Social History of Victorian Britain, 1830-1900*, (London, Fontana, 1988,) p. 140, 319. Walton, *Lancashire*, p. 187, 194; Alan J Kidd, *'Outcast Manchester: Voluntary Charity, Poor Relief and the Casual Poor 1860-1905'*, in Kidd and Roberts, *City Class and Culture*, p. 53.

9. Laqueur, *Religion and Respectability*, p.103,105,132; Walton, *Lancashire*, p. 185; Manchester Anglican Sunday School Minutes 27 Dec 1815, Chetham's Library, ref. A.6.5.
10. Mabel Tylecote, *The Manchester Mechanics' Institution 1824-50, in Artisan to Graduate*, DSL Cardwell, ed, (Manchester, Manchester University Press, 1974).
11. Hayes, *Raikes, the Pioneer*, pp. 15, 24; James Walvin, *Leisure and Society, 1830-1950*, (London, Longman, 1978), p. 86; Laqueur, *Religion and Respectability*, p. 186.
12. Snell, *The Sunday School Movement*, p. 126, 142.

Chapter 2: 1801-1818: The Early Years

Sources:
- Christopher Lee, *This Sceptered Isle*, Penguin, 1998.
- Alan Kidd, *Manchester*, Keele University Press, 1993.
- There is little primary evidence from the school for this period; David Stott apparently left no papers.
- Reports of the General Committee for the Management and Support of Sunday Schools of the Established Church on the present State of Sunday School 1788–1811. (Reports for the years 1797-1803 are not in the Bennett Street archive).

Footnotes:
1. *Lancashire Faces and Places*, 1910.
2. Gun Street Sunday School, the gift of Simeon Newton, became a long-lived Sunday school with its own interesting history.
3. *Bennett Street Memorials: A record of Sunday school work*, Manchester: Abel Heywood & Son, London: Simpkin,

Marshall & Co., 1831, address given by George Milner at the first Founder's Day.

4. Manchester Anglican Sunday School Minutes, June 1811, reference (A6.6) Chetham's Library, Manchester.
5. Benjamin Braidley's Diary: Bennett Street archive, ref M103/19/6/1.
6. *Bennett Street Memorials, 1831*, condensed from a sixteen page memorial of Simon Taylor.
7. All Lancashire mill towns had a summer 'Wakes week' when the mills stopped running and the entire town closed down and took a holiday. Manchester never did have a Wakes week but took Whit Week as its annual holiday. The Whit Monday bank holiday was replaced in 1971 by the Spring bank holiday.
8. Alan Kidd, *Manchester*, Keele University Press, 1996, p.50-52.
9. The Whit walks have recently (2013) been revived.
10. Manchester Anglican Sunday School Minutes, May 1801; April and June 1811 (reference A6.5 and A6.6) in Chetham's Library, Manchester.
11. *Like a Mighty Tortoise, A History of the Manchester Diocese*, Rev A J Dobbs 1978, Upjohn and Bottomley Printers Ltd., p. 146.
12. Holdsworth's mill later re-located to Reddish but the firm continued to support the school to the end.
13. Minutes of the Proceedings of the Subscribers and Trustees of the Sunday Schools under the Establishment, Bennett Street Manchester 1818–1820.

Chapter 3: 1818-1850: St Paul's Bennett Street Sunday School

Sources:
- Christopher Lee, *This Sceptered Isle,* Penguin, 1998.
- Alan Kidd, *Manchester*, Keele University Press, 1993, especially chapter III.
- Bennett Street archive: Minutes of the Teachers' and Visitors' Committee and Committee of Management; Annual Reports.

Footnotes:

1. Alan Kidd, *Manchester, p.96.*
2. Stuart Hylton, *History of Manchester,* Phillimore, 2003, p.81.
3. Bennett Street Annual Report 1842. 1851 census figures quoted in S J Davies, Classes and Police in Manchester 1829-1880, in Kidd and Roberts, eds, *City Class and Culture: Studies of Social Policy and Cultural Production in Victorian Manchester*, Manchester: Manchester University Press, 1985, p.34.
4. British Parliamentary Papers 1833: Factory Inquiry Commission on Ancoats, First Report, Employment of Children in Factories XX D1, 1833, p.p. 39-40.
5. Bennett Street Committee of Management Minutes 1847.
6. Kidd, *Manchester;* Hylton, *History of Manchester,* p.123.
6a. Exhibition 'Unseen Lowry' at the Lowry Centre Gallery, Salford, September 2013
7. Prior to the Whit Monday service the Collegiate Church actually removed glass from some of their windows to provide ventilation 'as may be thought necessary according to the state of the weather'. Manchester Anglican Sunday School Minutes 27 May 1807 (ref A6.5) in Chetham's Library, Manchester.
8. Rev Henry Taylor, Memorial to David Stott, *Memorials*, 1880, p.130.
9. Minutes of the Manchester Anglican Sunday Schools, October 1811, (archive ref. A6.6), in Chetham's Library, Manchester.
10. Ian Shaw, *Rev William Nunn and the Bennett Street Sunday School Manchester 1817-1824, Manchester Region History Review, xii 1998*, pp.27-34; Minutes of Bennett Street Trustee meetings 1824, M103/1/1; Minutes of the Manchester Anglican Sunday Schools, July 1824, (archive ref. A6.6), in Chetham's Library, Manchester.
11. Minutes of Visitors' and Teachers' Meetings, M103/1/2.
12. The day school is the subject of a separate chapter.
13. Whit Monday procession documents, (archive ref A.6.6), Chetham's Library, Manchester.

14. *Memorials*, 1880, p.29. The tea service is now in the safe-keeping of Manchester Cathedral and from time to time is on display there.
15. Memorials of David Stott and Benjamin Braidley, *Memorials*, 1880, p.24. An appreciation of both David Stott and Benjamin Braidley appears at the end of this chapter; the eulogy on the Stott grave is quoted in full.

David Stott Sources:

- *Bennett Street Memorials, 1880 and 1904.*
- D Brian Cooper: (David Stott's great-great grandson): *David Stott of Bennett Street Sunday School, Manchester Genealogist* Vol.2, No 1, 2006.
- *St Paul's New Cross Church Magazine*, November 1966.

Benjamin Braidley Sources:

- *Memorials, 1880 and 1904*, also *Report on Founder's Day 1895.*
- Benjamin Braidley Diary, archive ref: M103/18/6.
- James Philips Kay, *The Moral and Physical Condition of the Working Classes Employed in the Cotton Manufacture in Manchester*, 2nd edition 1832, (Manchester, E J Morten, 1969), p. 58.

Chapter 4: 1850-1870: The Heyday of the School

Sources:

- Christopher Lee, *This Sceptered Isle*.
- Alan Kidd, *Manchester*.
- Minutes of the Committee of Management.

Footnotes:

1. Alan Kidd, *Manchester*. Jonathan Schofield, *Manchester Then and Now*, Batsford, London 2009.
2. Schools Committee Annual Report 1851. *Memorials* 1904 p. 33.
3. *Memorials* 1880 p. 34.

4. J C Lockhart, 'Certain Legends of the Old School', *Odds and Ends Manuscript Magazine,* 1882. The full article was re-printed in *Bennett Street Memorials,* 1904. Lockhart recalled his childhood at the school in the 1850s.
5. A national society dating from the late 1840s established to promote abstinence among children.
6. *A Supplementary Book of Hymns and Songs for Home and School to which are added A Sunday School Service and a series of Home Prayers,* Manchester, St Paul's Sunday School Bennett Street, Sixth Edition 1896: Entered at Stationers; Hall, M103/19/12.
7. Quarterly Statistics 1855-1859 M103/8/9; Annual Report 1860. According to national statistics, in 1850 30% of males and 50% of females were unable to sign their name on their marriage register, G Sutherland in FML Thompson, *The Cambridge Social History of Britain, 1750-1950, Vol 3, Social Agencies and Institutions,* Cambridge, Cambridge University Press, 1990.
8. Presidential centenary address 1943; Literary and Educational Society minutes.
9. The volumes of the *Odds and Ends Manuscript Magazine* from 1855 to 1962 were the first Bennett Street archives to be offered to the Manchester Central Library in 1965 and they remain a primary source of writings by the people of the area during the nineteenth and twentieth centuries.
10. *Memorials* 1904, p. 71.
11. *Memorials* 1904 p. 34.

Chapter 5: 1870–1900: After the Education Act

Sources:
- Christopher Lee, *This Sceptered Isle.*
- Alan Kidd, *Manchester.*
- Minutes of the Committee of Management Annual Reports.
- *Bennett Street Memorials.*

Footnotes:

1. B A Redfern, *Memorials*, 1904 p. 58; Kidd, *Manchester*, p. 138; T Wyke in *The Church in Cottonopolis: Essays to mark the 150th Anniversary of the Diocese of Manchester*, eds. Chris Ford, Michael Powell and Terry Wyke, (Manchester, Lancashire and Cheshire Antiquarian Society, 1997), p. 338.

2. G Milner, *Memorials.*, 1880 p xlvii; William Hepworth Dixon, the editor of the *Athenoeum* 'one of the best known journals in England' had received his first education at Bennett Street as had Thomas Leary who went on to Manchester Grammar School and Oxford. He became editor of the *Rock* and subsequently a clergyman in London.

3. Founder's Day records: M103/19/2.

4. *The Quiver*, magazine published by Cassell & Co., London; *Memorials* 1904, p. 231; *Quiver*, Vol.1897 p. 383.

5. Annual Reports 1888, 1892.

6. Redfern, *Memorials* 1904 p. 239; Milner, *Memorials* 1880, p. 40.

7. Committee of Management minutes 1874, 1888; also miscellaneous printed papers concerning the men's class: M103/19/7.

8. Annual Report 1892; Redfern, *Memorials* p. 55.

9. *Manchester Guardian* 2 July 1889.

10. George Milner's notebook, St Paul's Literary and Educational Society archive: M/38/3.

11. Literary and Educational Society report in Annual Report 1888/89; *Memorials*, 1880, p.30; a conversazione is defined as 'a meeting, especially in the evening, for conversation and social recreation', *(Webster's Collegiate Dictionary)*.

12. Newscutting: Milner's speech at presentation of Humane Society certificates, May 1893, M103/19/8.

13. Redfern, *Memorials* 1904, p. 50

14. FML Thompson, *Rise of Respectable Society*, p. 252; Redfern, *Memorials*, 1904 p 46.

15. *Odds and Ends Manuscript Magazine*, 1882, re-printed in *Memorials*, 1904 p. 245.

16. Milner, *Memorials*, 1880, p 25.

17. Redfern, *Memorials*, 1904, p 47.

18. Industrial Exhibition Programme 1890, archive ref: M/103/19/7.

19. Womens Class report in Annual Report 1888.

20.   Shelley Rohde, *A Private View of LS Lowry*, London, Methuen 1987 p. 25.

Chapter 6: 1900-1914: The Centenary of the School

Sources:
- Christopher Lee, *This Sceptered Isle, Twentieth Century*, BBC and Penguin, 1999.
- Alan Kidd, *Manchester.*
- Minutes of Committee of Management.
- Annual Reports.

Footnotes:
1. Christopher Lee, *This Sceptred Isle, Twentieth Century*, p.p. ix, 1.
2. Alan Kidd, *Manchester,* p. 139.
3. Miscellaneous papers and Centenary Services leaflet: M103/19/7.
4. St Paul's New Cross Manchester Parish Magazine, April 1904, M103/19/11.
5. Centenary programme, M103/19/7 and Committee of Management minutes 1901.
6. *Certain Legends of the Old School.*
7. Programmes, pantomimes, plays, etc Archive ref M103/19.
8. St Paul's New Cross Manchester Parish Magazine, August 1905, M103/19/11.

Chapter 7: 1914-1918: The First World War

Sources:
- Christopher Lee, *This Sceptered Isle, Twentieth Century.*
- Alan Kidd, *Manchester.*
- Minutes of the Committee of Management and Schools' Committee.
- Trustee Meetings. Annual Reports.

Footnotes:
1. Alan Kidd, *Manchester*, pp.139,154, 166, 184, 223.

2. *Manchester City News*, Saturday 3 June 1916.
3. Annual Report 1916.
4. Roll of Honour M103/19/7.
5. *Manchester Faces and Places* 1891, 1901, 1905.
6. News Cuttings December 1914, M103/19/8.

Chapter 8: 1918-1939: The Interwar Years

Sources:
- Christopher Lee, *This Sceptered Isle, Twentieth Century*.
- Alan Kidd, *Manchester*.
- Minutes of the Committee of Management, the Schools' Committee and Annual Reports.

Footnotes:
1. *This Sceptered Isle*; Oxford bags defined as wide baggy trousers (Oxford English Dictionary)
2. Alan Kidd, *Manchester*, p. 216.
3. Bennett Street Schools Committee Annual Report 1919. No 2 room housed boys from age eleven upwards.
4. Thanks are expressed to Bill Gow (Scout Leader) for the above information on the scout troop.
5. *Manchester Evening News* 17 – 24 May 1926
6. Alan Kidd, *Manchester*, p. 228, 'The Sunday School Union Women's Hockey League had six divisions with an average of 11 teams in each'.
7. See separate chapter on the day school.
8. The appreciation of William Ashton has been compiled from the Minutes of the Committee of Management 1916, the Roll of Honour M103/19/7 and a torn and incomplete fragment of the Sunday School Magazine, 1934.

Chapter 9:[1843-1940: The Bennett Street Day School]

Sources:
- St Paul's Schools' Committee minutes; Annual Reports.

Footnotes:

1. Gillian Sutherland, in F M L Thompson, ed. *The Cambridge Social History of Britain 1750-1950, vol. 3, Social Agencies and Institutions,* (Cambridge, Cambridge University Press, 1990), vol 3, p. 127.

2. John K Walton, Lancashire: *A Social History 1558-1939,* (Manchester Manchester University Press, 1994), p. 194; Alan Kidd, 'Outcast Manchester:Voluntary Charity, Poor Relief and the Casual Poor 1860-1905', in Kidd and Roberts, eds, *City Class and Culture: Studies of Social Policy and Cultural Production in Victorian Manchester,* (Manchester, Manchester University Press, 1985 p.53; F M L Thompson, *The Rise of Respectable Society: A Social History of Victorian Britain, 1830-1900,* London, Fontana 1988, p. 140.

3. The position of the apostrophe reminds us that Bennett Street was only one of several Sunday schools originally attached to this church by the Manchester General Committee.

4. Terry Wyke, 'The Diocese of Manchester: An Introductory Bibliography', in Chris Ford, Michael Powell and Terry Wyke, eds, *The Church in Cottonopolis, Essays to mark the 150th Anniversary of the Diocese of Manchester,* Lancashire and Cheshire Antiquarian Society, Manchester 1997, pp. 284, 336.

Chapter 10: 1939-1945: The Second World War

Sources:

- Christopher Lee, *This Sceptered Isle, Twentieth Century.*
- Alan Kidd, *Manchester.*
- Minutes of the Committee of Management.
- The Schools' Committee and Annual Reports.

Footnotes:

1. Alan Kidd, *Manchester,* p. 187.

2. A member's eye witness account, written up in the Literary and Educational Society's *Odds and Ends Magazine 1940.*

Chapter 11: 1945-1966: Post War Decline

Sources:
- Christopher Lee, *This Sceptered Isle: Twentieth Century.*
- Alan Kidd, *Manchester.*
- Minutes of Committee of Management and of Trustee Meetings.

Footnotes:
1. Christopher Lee, *This Sceptered Isle: Twentieth Century*, pp. 267-9.
2. Thanks is expressed to Bill Gow (Scout Leader) for information on the scout troop.
3. BSSS = Bennett Street Sunday School.
4. Shelley Rohde, *A Private View of L S Lowry*, Methuen. 1979, p. 7.

Chapter 12: 1966: The Closure

Footnotes:
1. Minutes of Trustee Meeting, 20 September 1966.
2. *Manchester Evening News*, 25 October 1966.
3. *Bennett Street Magazine*, November 1966.
4. Manchester Diocesan Year Book.

A Brief Summary of Most Common Coinage in the Nineteenth Century

Coin	Colloquial Pronunciation	Value	Value in Symbol/Figures	Value in Decimal Currency	Description
Guinea	Gini	1 pound + 1 shilling	£1 1s 0d Also £1/1/-	£1.05	Gold coin. Similar to today's £1 coin, but half the thickness
Half a Guinea		10 shillings + sixpence	10s 6d Also 10/6, 10-6	52.5p	Gold coin – smaller than 1 guinea
Pound		20 Shillings	£1 0s 0d Also £1/-/-	£1.00	
Crown		5 Shillings	5s Also 5/-	25p	Silver coin - Size as per today's commemorative coins
Half a Crown		2 Shillings +sixpence	2s 6d Also 2/6	12.5p	Silver coin – largest coin in common usage but smaller than the crown.
Florin	Florin (as in Florid)	2 Shillings	2s or 2/-	10p	Silver coin – similar size to today's 50p piece, but round
Shilling	Shiling or bob	20 = 1 pound	1s or 1/-	5p	Silver coin – similar size to today's 10p
Sixpence	Sixp'nce	2 = 1 shilling	6d	2.5p	Silver coin – small, size between today's 5p and 10p
Three Penny Bit	Threp'nce	2 = Sixpence	3d	1.25p	Small silver coin similar size to today's 5p. Also a thick yellow 12 sided coin.
Penny		12 = 1 shilling	1d		Copper – Larger than any decimal coin
Half Penny	Hayp'ny	2 = 1 penny	½ d		Copper 'should be 1" diameter' (Harnsworth Universal Encyclopaedia)
Farthing	Farthing	4 = 1 penny	¼ d		Small copper coin similar to today's 1p

Index

Victoria, Queen   25, 58, 68, 71, 73, 86, 107, 133

Walker, Rev D E   118, 129
Wartime Conditions   124, 161-168
Welfare Provision   51, 67
Whit Monday   vii, viii, 20, 45 68, 73, 84, 100-106, 110, 113-114, 123,
         129, 131, 140, 145, 166, 181, 189, 190
Whit Week   19, 45, 68-69, 84-86, 113-114, 121, 123-124, 145-147,
         154, 166-167, 173, 176-177, 189
William IV   25, 29
Women   4, 81, 89-90, 97. 110, 115-116, 120-121, 133, 139, 149, 161,
         173-174, 178
Women's Suffrage Movement   107
Workman's Art Exhibition   69
Worsley, Lancashire   69
Worthington's   51

About the Author

Margaret Wendy Lees retired in 1996 after a forty year career divided equally between administration in Manchester's raw cotton trade and on the support staff of the Manchester School of Management, University of Manchester Institute of Science and Technology (UMIST), now the University of Manchester.

After retirement she enrolled for an MA in the History of the Manchester Region at the Manchester Metropolitan University, submitting a dissertation on '*A study of two large Sunday Schools in the Manchester region during the Victorian and Edwardian eras*'. The schools were Stockport Sunday School and Bennett Street Sunday School. She graduated in 2001.

She was the fourth generation of her family to be a scholar at Bennett Street Sunday School, her father Edmund Grundy Lees having also been a teacher, her grandfather Walter Lees a manager and her great grandfather John Grundy a manager and a Visitor.